Laura,
Thank you SO MUCH for
supporting me! ♡

THE LANGUAGE OF LOSS

THE LANGUAGE OF LOSS

NATALIE SANCHEZ

NEW DEGREE PRESS

COPYRIGHT © 2020 NATALIE SANCHEZ

THE LANGUAGE OF LOSS

ISBN 978-1-64137-825-3

For Dad, Mom, Dominic, Gabe, and Luke:
Words are timeless, and love is everlasting.
Through these pages, I hope you remember
that our family is forever.

CONTENTS

———

FOREWORD

———

Natalie Sanchez has all the right tools; an inquisitive mind, a quest for adventure, an evolving awareness of the balance of life and death. She asks important questions … a soul searcher on a journey of discovery to find her purpose, a desire to do something great.

In talking about her father, Natalie states "My Dad gave me a gift (of music) I know I can never repay." Nevertheless, she persisted. We bear metaphorical witness to the maestro's baton being handed from father to daughter. Long may they continue this songbird duet, this pas de deus. There is magic in this music, this legacy gift. Elton John spoke of such a gift when he sang "My gift is my song … and this one's for you." Clearly, this book is her song - offered lovingly and with gratitude to her late father. Debt repaid, with continuing interest. Something beautiful to help balance the sadness.

I'm honored to join the chorus and sing the praises of this grief-mirroring-love story. It is apparent Natalie's dad feels one of his own best songs is his daughter; a magnum opus that connects father and daughter for now and forever, an unbreakable bond that teaches us that love is, in fact, stronger than death. This is not a book about "the day the music died." It is about coming full circle; as the father's voice falls, the daughter's voice rises. Will it fly high, like a bird up in the sky? Read it and weep - you may discover your tears are equal parts heartbreak and joy. Again, balance.

Chapter by chapter, Natalie distills the chaos of her grief journey into her essential healing truth; a truth captured in Dan Fogelberg's classic ode to his father "Leader of the Band."

A beautiful story honoring a relationship between a daughter and her dad, the "leader of the band." This is not a book about death, but rather a story of life, a necessarily evolving relationship, and continuing love. Props to Natalie; YOU are a living legacy to the leader of the band. And this is your song.

-PATRICK DEAN, DIRECTOR OF WISCONSIN GRIEF
EDUCATION CENTER, WRITER, PHOTOGRAPHER,
THANATOLOGIST AT GRIEFWORK.COM

INTRODUCTION

———

Loss is one of those inevitably devastating human experiences that brings us to our knees. Chances are, if you're reading this, you already know that.

The idea that death can uproot our lives at any given moment is terrifying to me. I have learned that time is fleeting, and everything is only temporary. Our world can, without warning, spiral out of control, leaving only the wake of an unrecognizable future and our fragile memory of the past.

And what's even more terrifying is that this is all part of life.

The experiences of heartbreak and loss are deeply intertwined with the human experience. In fact, they are guaranteed. Traveling through life without ever feeling pain is virtually impossible. In a world where almost everything has a time and place, we can only expect to fall to our knees at one point or another. Loving anything comes with a hefty price, and most of the time, we are willing to pay it. Is the answer to close ourselves off from love?

Ever since I was a little girl, I've been a soul searcher. For the entirety of my life, I've been plagued by the question: "What is my purpose?" To most people, this question seems unfit for anyone to answer. It seems far too broad, too intimidating, too subjective to ever reach something close to a conclusion. But these words have been weighing on my heart from the moment I realized that, as human beings, we have potential.

I remember as a kid, I would pray to God and ask Him to "let me do something great." The sentiment seems so innocent and maybe even laughable now, but those same words still echo in the back of my head. I think, in part, my hunger for "something great" has driven me to become a creator—a creator in the word's many forms. It has fueled my unspoken rule of discovery, and for all the years of my existence, I have been aching for more.

My life remains contingent upon this grand question of purpose. Some days this question is subtler than others, but nevertheless, I continue to find myself restlessly searching for answers. Every moment of reflection leaves me wondering where I am going next.

After losing my dad, the grand and equivocal question of the universe only grew in complexity. The emptiness left me in a sort of daze somewhere between existential crisis and raw, paralyzing heartache. As death always does, the grief completely derailed my life. My beliefs, my experiences, my passions—everything changed. What was once an unadulterated perspective of the world suddenly became a disorienting crossroads.

Caught between the drawbacks of grief and the opportunity to grow, I realized my new perspective on life gave me two clear choices: sink into my pain or use it to construct the person I was always meant to become. The loss had transformed my life and its steady course but did not end it.

Whether we realize or not, losing someone sparks an internal metamorphosis that we can either nurture or ignore. This reshaping of the mind and soul allows us to mourn, but it also allows us to simultaneously weave our passions and pain into purpose. Where there is grief, there can be growth.

Grieving is a continuous process, one that involves falling, rising, moving forward, and repeating. Although this process never ends, it is necessary for growth. The falling reminds us that we are still capable of feeling and loving, that the loss is very much a part of our life. The rising is proof that life continues, but not separately from our pain. Joy and grief coexist in one breath, a juxtaposition between the two extremes that makes us human. Learning to embrace this combination brings forth a deep sense of meaning.

I often sit and imagine all the things I would say to a younger, more innocent, and much freer version of myself. All the things I would warn myself about, all the pain I would have to anticipate. I cannot seem to imagine what my younger self would have done if I knew that tragedy was on the brink of my future. If someone had warned me of all the obstacles ahead, I don't think I would have believed them. How could I? The life I had was not perfect, but looking back, it sure felt like it. I wish I had known how fleeting that bliss would be.

In a different light, I wonder what I might have thought if someone told me about all the good things yet to come. That because of the pain, I would evolve into a completely new human being, the one I was always meant to be.

I am not here to tell you a singular remedy for your pain exists—because it doesn't. Grieving isn't supposed to be linear, and it's definitely not supposed to fit into a universal paradigm of five steps. What I can tell you is that in that pain lies profound power—the power to cultivate growth.

As human beings, we have a limitless capacity for rediscovering a passion for life in our most joyful, most exciting moments. But what about the other extreme, when we are standing on the precipice of grief, staring into the dark abyss of loss itself?

When I unexpectedly lost my dad in March 2018, I felt this connection between heartache and purpose begin to blossom in the months following his death. I didn't know why, but my pain became the driving force behind my search for meaning, which seemed so counterintuitive. The profound loss of my dad catalyzed the loss of many other things: my interests, my happiness, even myself. Yet, simultaneously, I somehow developed an infinite hunger for living with intention.

At first, I thought my response was just a phase of the grieving process that would pass the second reality fully set in. Perhaps my craving for purpose was only a symptom of naiveté and misguided hopefulness. But instead, as I crawled along the journey, I found people and experiences that changed me, individuals I would not have otherwise met, and knowledge I could have never gained without grief. These people confirmed all speculations and made my reality crystal clear: loss breathed purpose into my life.

* * *

This book contains a collection of stories. Some are personal anecdotes; others are narratives of people who inspired me along the way. Although each one represents a different part of my experience and the lessons I have learned, they all hold a special place in my heart. These are the stories I think deserve to be told, not because they are extraordinary or even isolated incidents, but because they connect us as humans. People suffer every day, and loss is by far humanity's most universal form of pain. I have included these stories because they are conducive to my journey and hopefully to yours too.

Beyond the facts, statistics, or articles, real accounts of human experience cannot be encapsulated by research. Simply put, life is an amalgamation of stories: good times, bad times, and everything in between. This is the most precious gift we have: memories that propel us from one chapter to the next.

Through the pages of this book, I hope you realize that you can embark on the healing road. However, I want to clarify—healing is not synonymous with moving on. I think so often "healing" is misunderstood as a milestone in the grieving journey where we accept the loss, submit to our pain, and leave the grief behind us. But you already know there is no such thing as "moving on" from this journey. How could we? More importantly, why would we want to? Experiencing feelings so raw and real means we loved deeply and what we lost was of immense value.

What I mean by healing aligns pretty closely with the word's dictionary definition: the process of making or becoming sound or healthy again.[1] I don't want you to forget about your grief. I want you to nurture it in a way that allows you to form a healthy relationship between the very thing that breaks your heart and the passions that fill it with wonder. Whether you believe it or not, you are overwhelmingly capable of doing so.

When you read the stories in this book, remember that loss gives us the opportunity to love deeper and stronger than we ever have before. Understanding ourselves and the countless emotional hurdles we face along the way helps us realize who we are and who we are meant to become. It reminds us we have a purpose, and that purpose is good. Taking that emptiness and supplementing it with new hobbies, interests, and ideas can make the impalpable emotions of grief seem more concrete. Getting in tune with ourselves teaches us it is okay to feel. We live in a world where the idea of feeling is too often inundated with responsibilities and expectations, always pushed below the surface for the supposed sake of our strength . . . but we need to feel to survive.

Although pain is inevitable, we can find a way to make sense of that pain. Finding our purpose is powerful, it is healing, and it is our greatest expression of love for those we have lost. Why not carry out the rest of our life with intentionality? Why not seek meaning through our passions? And why not get out of bed every morning with the motivation to honor our loved ones while experiencing a life that is rewarding and wholesome? You can heal, you can grow, you can give; life is too short to do anything else.

---

1   *Merriam-Webster*, s.v. "heal," accessed February 8, 2020.

I am of course no expert on grief. I'm still learning, still searching. This book is not meant to be a cure or blueprint for living without someone you love; it is here to make grieving feel more like what it really is—love. I hope as you come with me on this journey, you find new ways to love those you have lost. I hope you find new reasons to get out of bed in the morning, reasons that inspire you to find new outlets, passions, and talents—things that seize you with joy and remind you to listen to your heart. But most of all, I hope as you read this book, you learn to navigate this difficult journey with everything already inside of you.

A MESSAGE IN MUSIC

As you'll come to know, music has become an inseparable part of my life, especially my grief. While I was writing this book, I found songs that inspired me, carried me, and pushed me to keep going when I wanted to throw everything into the garbage. So to share my dad's love of music and give this book another layer, I have included a suggested song at the end of every chapter. You can listen to them or you can pass over them, but know these songs have given life to many of the stories in these pages. If you choose to listen, I hope they resonate with you as much as they do with me. So, here you have it now, in music and in words . . . my story.

WITH LOVE ALWAYS,

NATALIE

grief is a crazy thing. i've come to understand that there is no one way in which grief manifests itself. it's imperfect and crippling and comforting and painful and confusing all at once. there is the grief that grips my heart, tightens my throat, and leaves me a mess on the floor. the kind where my stomach turns itself inside out and where my eyes run dry. there is the grief that seizes me in the middle of the night, where my dad is very much alive and my dreams are almost, just almost real enough, so that for those first brief and beautiful seconds, I think it is real. there is a quiet side of grief, the silent tears, the hidden pain, the heaviness that follows us like a dark cloud. and the laziness. no one ever warns you about the laziness. the days where the grief is so overpowering that I cannot even leave my bed to brush my teeth. there is the acceptance of grief. the waves come and we embrace them, because within the pain lies the remnants of our love. there are the hours where I could curl up in a ball and listen to his favorite songs because grief cannot be stifled. it needs to be felt. there is the grief that breaks through in moments, so soft and fleeting that I can swallow it. other moments where I have learned to hold it in my chest, until I can scream or sob or sing it away. there is the distracting nature of grief. the inability to focus, the uncontrollable wheel of thought, the desire to be anywhere but the present. grief is a monster. but it is also the calming waves of a quiet ocean and the promising sunrise reminding you that your love will carry you another day. grief is a journey, the darkest of roads, without a destination. but if we allow ourselves to walk along this path, with one foot in front of the other, we will walk miles with the one we love.

-natalie sanchez

Divine Savior Holy Angels High School Father Daughter Dance, 2017

PART I

FALLING

CHAPTER 1

THE END OF THE ROAD

———

No amount of words in the English language could even begin to describe the emptiness in my heart, but there is power in using words to express the impact of one's life on another.

—MARCH 17, 2018, A EULOGY TO MY FATHER

I opened the door to a tiny waiting room, my hands shaking, head spinning. I didn't know why I was there, but the painful knot in my stomach told me something was wrong, horribly wrong. As I stepped through the door, my mom stood with her arms outstretched, her face bearing an expression I did not recognize.

"I have to tell you that Dad died."

The words came tumbling out of her mouth, so foreign and shaky I didn't think they were real.

A surging range of emotions I had never felt before erupted from somewhere deep inside me, and my eyes instantly welled with tears.

"No, I don't believe you!" My voice was a silent scream, crying for help, begging for reality. As my eyelids closed over the nauseating hospital lighting, I collapsed into her arms. It was the first time in my life I had felt so hollow: an emptiness of words, feelings, or pain. It didn't make sense. This wasn't right. I was dreaming, wasn't I?

My mom wrapped her arms around me as I dug my face into her shoulder and continued to scream at the world. "I don't believe you!" The agony in my voice was so raw and unfamiliar. A wrenching pain began to form in my stomach and rise into my throat. My emotions felt invasive and unprecedented, a flood of uncontrollable thoughts and tears overwhelming my body.

I have to tell you that Dad died.

The inability to comprehend those words left me with no choice but to deny them. So I stood there, at war with my own instincts, refusing to believe the truth. I still could wake up; I had to be dreaming. But when my phone slipped from my hand and shattered on the cold tile floor, I realized it was all too real.

As I stood in the claustrophobic waiting room, with tears clouding my vision and the shock numbing my brain, I watched my world fall apart. I fell into an uncomfortable plastic chair and waited for the scene of loss to replay over and over before my very eyes. I braced myself as family member after family member walked into the room to hear the news.

That next hour felt too unreal to be a life that was mine. I felt like I was watching tragedy unfold through the eyes of someone else, like I was somehow trapped under the influence of a prolonged nightmare. I was light-years away from myself, out of touch with reality. So I sat, staring into space, aching and empty and numb to my core all at once.

In retrospect, that moment was mostly a blur. It was then I lost all concept of time and let the following minutes or maybe hours bleed together. In some ways, my memory of sitting in that uncomfortable plastic chair is just a recollection of fragments from that day. Fragments of my grieving family that will haunt me for the rest of my life.

My brother Dominic screaming, then taking off and running out of the hospital, down the street, away from reality.

My Uncle Eric sobbing in the chair next to me with his head hanging low and his hands folded over the back of his neck. "Not Paul," he whispered, "not Paul."

My Aunt Abby, my dad's younger sister, burying her face into my mom's shoulder and cupping her pregnant belly.

I half-consciously watched my grandparents, my cousins, my entire extended family filling up that tiny room as the minutes ticked by. Holding my other two little brothers in my arms, I squeezed their bodies as close as the world would let me. I didn't know if my inability to breathe was because of the crowded room or because I was suffocating under the heaviness of all our pain. Perhaps it was both.

When the social worker came into the room and opened the door so we could see him, I was oddly hopeful. I had no reason to believe and no desire to accept that my dad was truly gone. I repeated to myself again, This is just a dream. But when the door opened and I saw him lying there, I was faced with a piercing reality. Only hours ago, he had been in my room, talking, functioning, breathing. Now, he was motionless, resting in a makeshift emergency bed, with his eyes closed. When was the last time I had looked into his eyes? My entire world was swept out from beneath my feet, all in a matter of seconds.

All the color had left my dad's face: a face that was always filled with such color, kindness, and life. I collapsed onto a stool on his left side and touched him, thinking somehow it might bring him back. I ran my fingers through his hair. Kissed his forehead. Put my ear to his chest. Maybe his heart was still beating. Maybe the stroke never happened. This is a dream, I repeated to myself.

This is a dream. This is a dream. This is a dream.

As the rest of my family filtered into the room, I held his hand. I tried to memorize every callus and muscle, the exact weight of his hand in mine. I wanted to burn the feeling into my brain before I had to let go forever. His hand was still warm, the remnants of life lingering on his skin. The mere thought of dead bodies had always terrified me, but now, I could not stand the thought of leaving his side.

Everything I thought I knew about death seemed so wrong; a lifeless body was supposed to be gruesome and horrific—and it was—but for different reasons. The ugliness was not in what I saw, but in what I couldn't see. All parts of him were still so tender and familiar: soft strands of black hair falling over his forehead, peppery stubble lining his jawline, lips lightly pressed together like a peaceful deep sleep. Lifelessness was appalling, or at least it was supposed to be, but when the physicality of death is of your blood, of your being, the reason for your existence, it suddenly becomes too loving to be scary.

I clung to his hand, interlacing our fingers like I always did as a little girl. How was it fair, to lose his soul and his body all at once?

While I sat on the stool, still squeezing his hand and tracing its every outline, my mom and brothers gathered around him too. "Is there anything you guys want to say to him?" she whispered. It was the shell of a voice, one hollowed by the cruel aftermath of death, carrying the words of a woman with inhuman strength. That moment was my first realization of how death leaves us with no choice but to be strong, because grief is not about choices. Grief is about survival. It is about courage. It is about standing before the love of your life and praying you can be brave.

The five of us huddled around the hospital bed, staring, searching for the right language. What do you even say to express a lifetime of love with a matter of words?

C. S. Lewis once wrote, "We see the faces of those we know best so variously, from so many angles, in so many lights, with so many expressions, waking, sleeping, laughing, crying, eating, talking, thinking—that all the impressions crowd our memory together and cancel out into a mere blur."[2] That's exactly how I felt. Overwhelmed by my eighteen years of beautiful memories, I could hardly formulate a sentence. How do you prepare for such a moment? I didn't know grief could be so stagnant.

Standing there in a shock-induced trance, I tried to select the right words, if any existed, to say goodbye. The rest of my family told him their own "I love you's" and "thank you's" for their favorite memories, while I struggled to comprehend the absence of life inside his body. A few hours ago, he was here. Now, I had to fabricate a goodbye that was indicative of all the love he left behind.

A chaplain and a social worker stood in the corner while we huddled around my dad. Despite their kindness, it took everything inside me to restrain myself from screaming at them. Consumed by grief, I found their politeness off-putting. Their courteous smiles and willingness to help felt invasive and rehearsed. I knew they were doing their jobs, but my world had been robbed, and

---

2   C. S. Lewis, *A Grief Observed*.

I couldn't let my time be stolen too. If this was the last time my family would ever feel whole, I wanted us to be alone.

After almost everyone had arrived, somehow we all ended up in a crowded, lopsided circle and attempted to fumble our way through a prayer. Again, we couldn't seem to begin.

"Paul always said the prayer," Aunt Abby sniffled through a laugh, suppressing tears and wiping her eyes. She was right; he did. If we couldn't even start a simple prayer without my dad, I wondered how we would even begin to make it through life. We mumbled an "Our Father," and then the social worker helped my mom cover his palm in some paint so we could have his hand-print. I stared at my family, red-eyed, exhausted, and shocked. My heart was so numb I wasn't sure I would ever feel again.

The rest of that hour left me in a hypnotic state, where everything seemed artificial. The off-white hospital hallways, my beating heart, even the murmur of my family members embracing one another—I was convinced it was all an illusion. I drafted a message to my friends, paused to think whether text was an appropriate way to tell them, and sent it anyway. Seeing it in words nauseated me, so I put my shattered phone in my pocket, secretly hoping no one would respond. Receiving an answer meant it was real.

When I walked out of the parking lot that night and saw a glowing sliver of the moon, I wondered if he could see it too. I wondered if angels ever missed what they left behind. I wondered why I felt so numb.

But, most of all, I wondered when I would wake up.

A MESSAGE IN MUSIC
"Repeat Until Death" by Novo Amor

Before

natalie   My Mom   Me   My Dad   Dominic   Gabe

This is a drawing my youngest brother, Luke, ten years old at the time, drew to depict the way he felt.

After

CHAPTER 2

EDELWEISS

---

*Your drums haven't been touched in months. Maybe because
it feels wrong to play music so irreplaceable or maybe because
you truly were the heartbeat of our home.*

—JULY 6, 2018, A LETTER TO MY FATHER

Music has always been deeply ingrained in my life, but it
wasn't until my dad's passing that I fully realized its transformative nature. Growing up, we always had something playing
through our living room boom box. My dad's prized CDs
became a soundtrack of sorts for my childhood. Rush, The
Police, The Beatles, The Rolling Stones, Journey, The Outfield.
Pretty much every popular '80s and '90s rock band was in
my repertoire by the time I was ten years old.

When he passed away, music taught me how inescapable
the pain of grieving was. It was everywhere; his favorite songs
played in Target aisles, coffee shops, elevators, and seemingly
every radio station I flipped through. They were in movie sound-
tracks, grocery stores, high school dances, soccer game warmup
playlists, dancing in my head each time I started to daydream.

The first five seconds of a Phil Collins song instantly catapulted me into a time and place from my past, a memory flooding back of him drumming on the steering wheel. I could envision his calloused musician's fingers pounding the dashboard and then my shoulder, as I flinched and smiled and rolled my eyes in the passenger's seat. "I'm cold," I said to him, which always received a "Pretty soon it's gonna be winter—enjoy this while you can." Then I shivered through the autumn air, with all the windows rolled down and our silver Honda Odyssey proudly vibrating with "You Can't Hurry Love."

At prom, I found myself slumped on a bench outside the venue, surrounded by my best friends, tuning out the EDM music from the ballroom. Staring into the black river and hazy stars, we talked about nostalgia and grief and favorite memories. We could hear "Don't Stop Believin'," and suddenly we were running. Suddenly I was crying and singing and dancing while I belted the lyrics to the first song he taught me on the piano.

Then there was Van Halen, a musical time capsule of my childhood. My dad had somehow effortlessly replicated the masterpiece "Eruption" on an acoustic guitar. Mesmerized by his dexterity, I had sprawled on the bed, unblinking through its entirety. He seamlessly transitioned to "Here Comes the Sun"; I asked him to sing, and he always did.

For years, music had been my escape, but now I couldn't run to my haven of songs without the grief consuming me. Everything served as a reminder of the gaping hole in my heart, and music became a mirage of the man I could never get back. When I tried to escape its grasp on my memory, it felt like betrayal. Music and my dad and me were one, another vital organ I could not remove.

Because escaping suffering is so temporary, I soon realized all I could do was move with my grief. There was no moving on, no moving from, no leaving behind or getting over. When we lose someone, our only choice is to learn how to live alongside that perpetuating emptiness.

Although nothing could fill that space, I found something inherently natural about the way joy and grief began to coexist. Something about listening to my dad's favorite songs and fumbling my way through some ukulele chords taught me to let the pain take its course. When the waves of grief are calm, I let the music lift me up; when the waves feel like more than I can handle, I try not to resist them and instead cling to the songs that keep me above the water.

I thought losing my dad meant losing music too. I now know that losing him gave me the strength to delve even deeper into my passions. When you start focusing more on welcoming emotions rather than escaping them, you will discover a greater capacity to understand what you feel.

Allow everything inside you to shape your creative processes, your decisions, and your mindset. That pain is not an intruder; it belongs with you. Despite what we are indoctrinated to believe about grief, heartbreak gives us the greatest opportunity to grow.

SING FOR ME?

"Dad, I want to learn how to play the ukulele." I tapped him on the shoulder as he sat at his usual spot in front of the computer. He was scrolling though Penguinmagic.com, his favorite website for buying magic tricks and gimmicks.

"Really?" He turned around with a smile stretching across his entire face.

I knew my dad too well. Inside, he was ecstatic. Music was one of his greatest passions, and my budding interest was nothing less than a parenting dream come true.

"You do?" He leaned back in his chair, slowly breaking his gaze from the computer like a world leader plotting his next moves. Rubbing his fingers together with a devious smile, he couldn't hide his excitement. For him, any reason to go to Guitar Center was good enough.

Five minutes later, I was sitting in the passenger's seat of our green Ford Explorer, on my way to get a ukulele.

Something about wandering around the music shop always brought out my dad's childlike spirit. I followed him around the store as he walked through all the aisles, picking up every single item on display. He sat down to strum the most expensive guitars, toggle with the controls on the newest keyboards, and pound on the flashiest drum sets. He was in his element, and he couldn't be stopped.

"That," he said, pointing to a glossy, bright red electric guitar, "is my dream guitar right there. A Gibson ES-335." He leaned in closer and teased, "You can tell your mom that's what I want for Christmas." I squinted to read the monstrous price tag and made a note on my phone: Gibson ES-335. The note was for me. One day, when I was much older, I was going to buy it for him. A potentially good retirement gift, I thought to myself.

When we finally reached the wall of ukuleles, my dad tested each one. He wanted the fit, the shape, the sound, the wood, even the material of the strings to be just right.

"How about this one?" He handed me a medium-sized, darker-grained ukulele. I turned it over and felt its every groove, trying to mimic his meticulous selection process. When I looked up to tell him that it was perfect, he was already on the other side of the room sifting through instructional books. He came back a few minutes later with an entire stack. I could sense his anticipation as he flipped through each book and showed me exactly what songs I needed to learn. There was Bob Marley, The Beatles, two separate books by The Lumineers, and at least five more buried under his other arm.

"Dad, I don't need all of these!" I was just a beginner, and all these materials seemed a little too ambitious.

He was glowing. "Just take them." He smiled and handed me a tuner, capo, stand, and a case. "Oh, by the way," he gestured to the ukulele, "that one doesn't have an amp jack, but I think that's a good one to get you started. We can always get another one once you get good, but—"

"Dad, I love it," I interrupted.

We went home, and without hesitation, he drilled a mount to the wall in my room so I could have my new little instrument on display.

Soon I became obsessed with playing the ukulele. I would come home from school and race up to my room to practice the few chords I knew. While sitting cross-legged on my bed, I tried to follow along with a YouTube video on my laptop, sometimes catching on, sometimes failing, but it was cathartic either way. I would repeat verses of songs until my fingers were sore, the streetlights lit up, and a persistent sense of guilt told me it was time to start my homework.

My dad was keen on nurturing this budding interest. One night, he impulsively bought the two of us tickets to a ukulele concert (yes, that is a thing) to see Jake Shimabukuro, a rising ukulele virtuoso. It was the most ridiculously fantastic concert, with this genius of a musician somehow filling an entire auditorium with a lively "Bohemian Rhapsody," using only a four-string ukulele.

"Are you gonna play like that some day?" he whispered in my ear during the show. I shook my head and sarcastically raised my eyebrows, but deep down, a sincere, inner voice, was mumbling "yes." Unintentionally, my dad always planted these little seeds of certainty. His confidence in my capabilities felt like the call to a challenge, so I spent the following months holed up in my room, trying to master my new instrument.

Every now and then, my dad would pop into my room and gesture for me to hand him my ukulele. It was his way of checking on my progress to see if his musical enthusiasm was still rubbing off on me. Purely by ear, he would pluck a quick verse to a song, hand it back, and say, "Let me see what you got." I would usually play a few chords from one of the songs I had learned before he prodded me: "Okay, now I want to hear you sing it."

I was always too hesitant to sing. It wasn't embarrassment or shyness, but a specific reluctance rose in me whenever someone was watching. Almost every night, he asked me to sing, and I always sent him away.

AN ETERNAL LULLABY

I sat cross-legged on my bed, staring at my ukulele on the wall and regretting every moment I didn't sing for him.

It didn't seem possible that he was gone. Three days had passed, and my heart was still numb. I kept replaying those moments in my head, the ones when he was still so vibrant and real. Memories of him singing "Edelweiss" from *The Sound of Music* kept finding their way to the surface of my mind, as if my life—my past—were flashing before my eyes, a constant reel of every moment we ever shared before he left. Although I knew he didn't choose to leave, his death felt so much like abandonment. No goodbye, not even a warning, just a quiet departure from one realm to the next.

I could still hear his voice so clearly, and I was terrified I might forget it one day. I closed my eyes and was suddenly five years old, tucked neatly under my covers, on the brink of a deep sleep. My dad's lullaby floated through my bedroom, with his calming baritone voice drifting through the house and into my dreams.

He always changed the lyrics. Instead of "homeland" he always sang, "Bless my Natalie forever." As a kid, I remember thinking those were the actual words . . . until, of course, I saw *The Sound of Music* and had to accept that "homeland" didn't sound as cool as my name.

With his calming voice and lyrical revisions, the song had always sent me off to sleep in a matter of minutes. Sometimes he rubbed circles on my back or traced a finger down my nose. As a child, this nighttime routine was foolproof, but even as I grew older, he liked to sing to me. He would creak open the door, sink into the bed next to me, and serenade my sleepy mind. For most of middle school and high school, I rejected these so-called "embarrassing" lullabies, but on those rare occasions when I let down my inhibitions, I let him sing to me. On those nights, he would always stay a while longer, relishing the moment before I remembered I was too old.

Still staring at the ukulele on my wall, I envisioned my dad cradling his newborn in a rocking chair. I could see him carrying his toddler up the stairs and into bed. I pictured him poking his head through the door to see his teenage daughter sleeping, missing the nights where he could hold her. Just as my dad had sent me to sleep with his songs, I was determined to give him a sort of eternal lullaby. Music could be my peaceful farewell to him, the goodbye I never got to give, and "Edelweiss" felt like a fitting song.

I trod down the stairs to my mom, unsure of what I even intended to ask. I had already committed myself to a eulogy, but now I knew that I had to sing.

At first, she was hesitant. Sitting in our living room, having coffee with a friend, she cocked her head as if she didn't recognize me. I hardly recognized me. My mom rarely heard me sing, because I never did . . . for other people, at least. Not for my family, not for anyone. And now, I wanted to sing in front of an entire church of people, on a day when my emotions could paralyze me.

Her friend chimed in and said that, most likely, I would not be able to sing a nonreligious song at a Catholic service. Apparently, a friend of hers had tried before and been unsuccessful. I could feel a sharp pain welling up inside me. This was my dad; I should get to choose how I wanted to honor him. Tears pooled in my eyes, and I took cover in our basement, screaming hysterically into my palms and waiting for the wave to subside.

Fortunately, our parish priest, Father Charlie, lovingly welcomed the idea. Later that night, he told my mom over the phone I could sing "Edelweiss," so on St. Patrick's Day, I slipped on a black dress (one I had borrowed from a friend so I never had to see it again), haphazardly put on some waterproof mascara, dragged my ukulele down the stairs, and climbed in our minivan to face the end of the world.

When the service started, I sat at the front of the church near the lectern, while my Uncle Brian delivered the first part of the eulogy. It was a curious perspective to be facing all the people who had come to pay their respects to my dad. The church was packed almost to its 1,000-person capacity. People were crammed in the aisles, the balcony, and every single pew. I was overcome with awe.

After both my uncles had finished their eulogies and I delivered mine, they walked across the altar with me to the group of chairs surrounding my ukulele.

The church was eerily quiet. I had never felt so many eyes on me in my life, their faces watching my every move as I picked up the ukulele and gently slung it over my shoulder. I put one hand on its neck, the other draped over its body, my fingers ready to play the first chord.

A sea of faces. Some crying, some smiling, some doing both with a simultaneous expression of pity and concern. What if I messed this up? I took a deep breath, leaned in toward the microphone, and started to strum.

The strange thing about the following two minutes of my life was that I felt nothing but peace. I had been nervous and shaky earlier that day, but when I started playing, I just felt a room overflowing with love. My uncles sat on either side of me, sources of moral support guiding me through the song. In some places my strumming was off and my voice trembled, but I did not care. I was doing what I needed to do. For my dad. For me.

It was another strange position to be facing the congregation and hearing my voice reverberate through the church. My vocal cords seemed to move on their own, my fingers transitioning through each chord without much thought. While my muscle memory momentarily took over, I let my mind wander to take in the surroundings, encoding the image of the church into my brain.

My dad's casket before the altar, the stained-glass windows above the organ, a woman clinging to a box of tissues. I could see my mom embracing my brothers, extending her arms to wrap around all three of them. Never once had I seen my grandpa leave his nursing home bed, but there he was, coherent speech stolen by a stroke, softly sobbing in his wheelchair. In a subconscious observation of my shattered world, I strummed an extra interlude to breathe.

After I played the final chord, I stood up and embraced my uncles. We held each other for a little bit before heading back to our seats in the pews. Everyone clapped, but my thoughts drowned out the applause. I had made it through the song, and that was what mattered. Maybe because I was still so numb, but maybe because something came over me in those two minutes, and maybe that something was my dad.

I hardly cried during that next hour, until a whisper of a voice surfaced through my thoughts. In the back of my head, I could almost hear his smile: "Nat, I'm so proud of you."

I trudged out of the church, feet heavy, heart heavier. I watched as they gently moved that dreadful wooden box into a big black car. The sun was bright. The sky was blue. I still thought I was dreaming.

A MESSAGE IN MUSIC
"Leader of the Band" by Dan Fogelberg

CHAPTER 3

THE HEARTBEAT
OF OUR HOME

———

*I can't sleep. The house is too quiet without you. The silence
is absolutely deafening.*

—APRIL 30, 2018, A LETTER TO MY FATHER

When I reflect on my life before my dad's passing, certain
moments replay over and over in my head. Sometimes, these
moments flood back with hints of guilt—times when I felt
annoyed, indifferent, ungrateful—an unfortunate culmination of the emotions that make us human. If you've lost
someone, you know what I'm talking about. The moments that
make you wonder if everything you said and did was enough.
We dissect. We overanalyze. We forget we are fallible creatures
with an enormous capacity for mistakes. This is what grief
does: it weighs on us with guilt, convincing us our love was
insufficient. Grief sits in the pit of our stomach, twisting our
memories with doubt, anger, and worst of all: regret.

However, regret is an inescapable part of life. It comes with every twist and turn of the journey, every minute when we are forced to choose. It comes with pain. And despite my dreams to live in a world completely free of regret, I have my own set of wishes to change what could have been.

My heaviest regret is something seemingly arbitrary and innocent: sleeping . . . choosing to snooze my alarm and close my eyes on the last day of my dad's life. My final memory of him is solidified in my brain. His light knock on the bedroom door. The struggle to open my eyes in my hazy, half-asleep state. Nodding on my pillow as he said something I can't recall. Although the memory is muddled, regret sharpens its soft edges.

I can recall the thoughts floating through my mind. I considered asking him to give me a guitar lesson, to go out to lunch, or to walk around the block, but I consciously decided to sleep instead. I could have chosen to get out of bed. I could have savored the last hours of his life, maybe even caught it on video.

Could have is a dangerous phrase. Imagining the possibility of something unalterable in the past leads our minds to dark places. Although it's easy to look back on those moments and examine every second we didn't spend in gratitude, we should just accept the moment for what it was. Sometimes, the unexceptional qualities of a memory are what make it so distinct. Fully embracing the moment in all its potential flaws and ordinary qualities will tell you that what you had was real.

RHYTHMS OF THE NIGHT

It was two in the morning. I groaned, rolled over, and sat straight up in my bed. Sleeping was a lost cause. The sound always carried from our basement, and I could hear my dad's passionate drum solos as if I were three feet away from him. I had two tests the next morning, but I had given up on falling asleep. Every time I tried to close my eyes, all I heard was the clashing of the cymbal and snare two floors below me.

"It's so loud!" I yelled from my room, hoping he would somehow hear me over his attempts to play along with Rush's iconic "Tom Sawyer" drum solo. Even from my bedroom, I could tell he was in his element. Now fully awake, I decided to go investigate.

"It's so loud," I complained, peering around the doorway. My dad's midnight drumming wasn't anything I hadn't seen before; this was a usual occurrence in our house. I tried to direct his attention toward me, but my dad was fixated on his drums. He was laughing as he bobbed his head up and down to the beat. "Daaaaaad!" I yelled over the deafening rhythm.

He just kept playing. I was sleep-deprived and annoyed, but a small part of me was suppressing a laugh. I sat down on the couch and waited for him to finish his drum solo; I knew he was not going to leave a musical masterpiece like this unfinished. So I sat and watched my dad, a king behind his fortress of instruments, walled into his precious corner of the basement by two sets of drums, a keyboard, display of amplifiers, and shiny electric guitars. Excited to see that he now had an audience, he twirled and flipped his drumsticks, banging on his sparkling blue Ludwig drum set like he was Neil Peart himself.

"Are you almost done?" I pleaded, trying to hide any signs of amusement from my face. He smirked at me and milked the last minute of his one-man performance, rapping every surface, kicking the bass drum, embellishing some of the rhythm with his hi-hat and cowbell. This grand finale ended with two drumsticks flying in the air and landing perfectly in his hands for the very last beat.

"How does that sound?" He grinned, slightly out of breath.

"Good," I said, raising my eyebrows in teenage indifference.

"You'll appreciate me one day when I'm gone," he said, laughing.

"Okay, sure." I smiled, half-teasing, half-grateful he was finally finished. And with that, I crawled upstairs to my bedroom and fell right asleep.

EMPTY SOUND

The drums looked lonely. A thin layer of dust had accumulated on the surface, and a few drumsticks were strewn across the floor exactly as he had left them. My mom had said my dad was the heartbeat of our home. I squeezed past all his instruments, careful not to upset the arrangement by an inch, and sat down in the swivel chair.

The drumsticks felt heavy in my hand. I loosened my wrists for a few experimental taps on the snare, trying to mimic his fast, fluid movements. 1-e-and-a-2-e-and-a-3-e-and-a, I counted to myself, attempting to recall the only drum lesson he ever gave me. I knew it was some sort of method to keep the tempo, but anything beyond the counting chant had escaped my mind.

My patience was wavering. The gentle, controlled rhythm was short-lived and quickly grew into loud, angry fits of frustration. I wasn't drumming anymore; I was fruitlessly trying to fill the silence with the sound that made my house feel like home.

Giving up, I wandered to the other side of our basement, feeling compelled to pick apart his meticulously curated bookshelf. It had books of every kind: coaching manuals, instructional guides for magic tricks, classic literature, music magazines. I rifled through his favorites: the works of Ayn Rand, C. S. Lewis, Mark Twain, Paulo Coelho. Toward the end of the row was a thick paperback with the image of a single motorcycle driving down an empty desert road. *Ghost Rider: Travels on the Healing Road,* the cover read, by Neil Peart.

I pulled the novel from its place and leafed through the pages. Neil Peart was an author? My dad had always ensured that my brothers and I were well-versed in all things music, including our knowledge of "the greatest drummer in the world." However, he had never once mentioned anything about Neil writing a book. As I read the back cover, I was shocked to learn that Neil was a survivor of loss himself; in the span of only ten months, he had lost both his wife and only daughter.

An instinctual hunch of sorts told me to open the book. I sat on my basement floor, surrounded by a pile of my dad's favorite historical works, and started to read.

THE GHOST RIDER

The book opened with a brief anecdote on a dark, rainy morning, where Neil packed a few belongings and hopped on his motorcycle to begin his journey alone. As he departed from his house in Canada, Neil described the night he lost his daughter.

It was early August in 1997, and Neil's successful career as a drummer in the band Rush had been continually gaining momentum after the *Test for Echo* Tour. Neil had been mindlessly watching a documentary when the town's local police chief pulled into the driveway and stepped inside.

"Bad news. Maybe you'd better sit down," the chief said.

Neil's wife Jackie sank to kitchen floor as they read the words on the paper: "single car accident" and "dead at the scene." Their nineteen-year-old daughter Selena had been killed on her way to start university in Toronto.

As Neil described the following weeks where family and friends filtered through the "House of Mourning," Jackie was inconsolable. He watched his wife descend into the perils of heartbreak, while he shielded his own soul from the pain. Every young woman triggered grief for Jackie. "I would just flinch and turn away from such associations," he wrote, "but Jackie remained raw and vulnerable, unable to protect herself from the horror of memory."

Although Neil tried to take care of his wife with loving gestures and distractive trips to beautiful getaways, Jackie fell deeper and deeper into a paralyzed, depressive state. "It was like witnessing a suicide brought on by total apathy," Neil said. "She just didn't care."

In January of that year, less than five months after Selena's passing, with this indifference for life, Jackie received a diagnosis of terminal cancer. Neil wrote, "The doctors called it cancer, but of course it was a broken heart, and a second nightmare began."

After a final vacation together in Barbados, Neil watched his life fall apart, with his wife "slipping away both mentally and physically, until a series of strokes brought a relatively merciful end."[3]

---

3   Neil Peart, *Ghost Rider: Travels on the Healing Road.*

Only a few pages into the book, I was staring blankly at the words, wondering how anyone could endure a tragedy like this. I was struggling with one loss, but two? And the only two people in his family . . . both gone in a matter of months? I knew Neil Peart was a drumming prodigy and the lyrical mastermind behind most of Rush's lyrics, but I suddenly held a deeper respect for this man my dad had always idolized.

The sudden, unbearable emptiness in Neil's life left him with no choice but to survive. Unlike Jackie, who had "surely willed her death," Neil wrote that he "felt armored with some kind of survival instinct, some inner reflex that held to the conviction 'something will come up.'" Two months after Jackie's death, he sold his house, packed a few necessary belongings, and left for somewhere, anywhere, on his motorcycle. "I was now setting out on my motorcycle to try to figure out what kind of person I was going to be and what kind of world I was going to live in. . . I soon came to think of it as the Healing Road. At the time, there was no way of knowing if traveling would 'work' for me, especially alone, but it proved to be the best remedy so far."

Meanwhile, he told Geddy and Alex, the other two band members of Rush, to "consider him retired." Neil felt nothing for music; he had been devoid of any desire to continue with the band.

Over the next fourteen months, he took a solitary journey across 55,000 miles, from Quebec to Alaska, down the coasts and eventually into Mexico and Belize, searching for a will to live.

Throughout the book, Neil referenced the need to nurture "his little baby soul," which he described as "a sputtering life force, a meager spirit, as though I cupped my hands around a guttering candle." While reading, I found myself feverishly circling entire paragraphs at a time. Neil had a way with words, and with each new chapter, I could feel his wisdom speaking to me. Our losses were wildly different, but his quest for hope on the "Healing Road" seemed so much like my own perspective. I, too, could sense a burning essence inside me, and I was determined to keep that "little baby soul" alive in whatever way I could.

In great detail, Neil's book traced the tales of his personal odyssey, a difficult search for meaning from somewhere deep inside himself. Through hundreds of cities, motels, and desolate roads, Neil carried his grief across continents. "I wasn't always feeling 'better' as the process of grieving oscillated," he wrote, "even through each day, from a little better to a little worse, from total existential despair to those occasional rays of hope and interest, which was definitely a spark of healing."[4]

I was already underlining and doodling stars around that word: oscillated. I refused to categorize grief under a universal model of five steps, because pain like this wasn't linear . . . it was a random, imperfect cycle that would never end. The days fluctuated, in no specific order, from the more placid and peaceful ones, to the raw and perpetuating brokenness. Grieving was unpredictable; all types of days were guaranteed to make their rounds, but you never knew what kind of day you were going to have each morning. So, naturally, Neil's interpretation resonated with me.

Along the way, Neil journaled about his travels, rising to powerful realizations about life and rediscovering his purpose.

---

4   Ibid., (26)

After fourteen long, transformative months, he returned home. Shortly after, he met a woman named Carrie, whom he eventually married. Labeled as his "real angel of redemption," Carrie encouraged Neil to return to the music scene. In January 2002, he began working again with Geddy and Alex in Toronto to compose a new Rush album, *Vapor Trails*.[5]

The songs in this album are based on Neil's experience. Nearing the end of the book, I froze. I thought of all those nights when my dad had dragged me to our desktop computer to watch videos of Neil drumming. He would play through several lengthy clips of Neil spinning in his 360-degree drum setup, wearing his iconic black tubeteika hat and tossing his sticks into the air like a sweaty circus performer.

"Look," my dad would say. "It's the best drummer in the world." If I showed any signs of disinterest, he would quickly click to the next video and eagerly wait for my validation. I never really understood the magnitude of Rush's success, let alone Neil's talent for drumming and writing. I had always thought that my dad's childlike fascination with Neil Peart was just a result of his uninhibited passion for music, but now I could see that his appreciation was rooted in something much deeper. Turning to the final page of the book, everything made sense. Neil was a drummer, a writer, and a fighter with heart, and those qualities are what my dad loved about this musician.

"As I stood on the Santa Monica Pier, the unofficial route end of Route 66, the 'Ghost Road,' I saw that it was a fitting place to entertain the sudden realization that the Ghost Rider's road ended there too," Neil wrote. "I was growing into a

---

5   Ibid., (456)

man again, with joy and meaning into my life, passing the days and nights in a place where I belonged."[6]

On the final page of the book, with a line that gave me chills, he wrote:

"Dedicated to the future, with honor to the past."[7]

THE HEARTBEAT OF HEAVEN

I spent the following months obsessing over Neil Peart and his creative ingenuity. Binge-watching interviews, documentaries, and live shows, I became engrossed with his story. Learning more about this man felt like I had discovered a treasure of my dad's existence, as well as a puzzle piece to my own grieving process. I admired Neil; his year of travel, reflection, and self-expression had given him entirely new insight into life.

And then, exactly one year and ten months after my dad's passing, Neil died. Sixty-seven years old. Brain cancer. It was all over the news. His death felt so personal for someone I had never met, but I guess that's what writing can do. Ghost Rider connected me with his loss and reawakened my love of language. Neil represented a small piece of my dad, and now he was gone, too.

I was overcome by an image of the two of them meeting each other in Heaven. I could see my dad elbowing his way to the front of the line, introducing himself, then begging to do a drum solo with Neil. I could hear the angels cheering, singing, rallying around them, as my dad outdid himself on a shiny drum set next to his idol, a new

---

6   Ibid., (457)
7   Ibid., (460)

best friend. I could almost hear their rhythm, a cohesive, celestial beat of passionate drumming and ethereal voices, blending in one eternal song.

A MESSAGE IN MUSIC

"Tom Sawyer" by Rush

CHAPTER 4

SHARING THE GOOD

———

I don't think grief is necessarily bad. I think it is the memory of the soul, the heart's way of continuously giving love, and recognizing the beauty of what we once had.

—JANUARY 9, 2019, A LETTER TO MY FATHER

The only connection Jen Hale and I shared was our grief and an itching desire to do something with our pain. We were both suffering from recent losses, and we both had decided to write a book.

I so clearly remember that first phone call, dialing her number and nervously anticipating her voice on the other end. While pacing around my dorm room, I was anxiously picking at my nails, waiting to share the most intimate parts of myself with a stranger hundreds of miles away. We had never met and never spoken, but our editor Stephen had connected us, in the hopes that we could discuss our experiences and bond over the struggles of writing a book.

Her voice was instantly calming. She was friendly and gracious, equally interested in my experience of loss as I was in hers. After only a few minutes of small talk, we began to open up to one another. Sharing with her felt natural . . . and necessary. I could already sense we were going to develop something special.

As we exchanged stories, I found myself increasingly captivated by her strength. Jen was working through her own set of obstacles, but she also possessed a unique mindset grounded in positivity. She told me about her struggles, her triumphs, and the newfound perspectives that brought her to share her experience.

Without even seeing her face, I felt a strong connection to Jen and her story. Something about her words and her intentions felt inherently relatable. We were living different losses and grieving different people, but the heartache was all too similar. It was the kind of heartache fueled by love, the kind that was debilitating, perplexing, and insurmountable. Jen had recently lost her mother, and her story resonated with me. After just one phone call with this woman I had never met, I wondered why we felt so connected, and why I felt so understood.

Over the coming months, Jen and I continued to share stories with one another through a sequence of cathartic phone calls. We talked about the complexity of putting our reality into words: things like writer's block, stubborn imposter's syndrome, and grief-induced nervous breakdowns. While navigating my own writing journey, Jen was always there. We cried to each other, venting when we felt defeated and celebrating tiny triumphs along the way. Writing was hard, writing about death was even harder, and writing about a personal death—one you lived and were still living—created a giant, tangled web of unfathomable emotions.

I had seen compassion in its many forms after my dad's death. The visual representations of kindness never failed to amaze me: sympathy arranged neatly on a flawless cookie platter, consolation wrapped up in a warm hug, condolences pouring from the cards piling up on our kitchen counter. I had seen people become their best selves, and it was beautiful, but for so long, I had been craving understanding. With Jen, there was no need for the long letters and the flowers and the casseroles. Just talking and knowing that she understood was a powerful gift itself.

I like to think that blessings often mask themselves in people, the ones who come to us when we least expect them. Although Jen lived in Maryland and we only talked via phone, I considered her a close friend. The friendship Jen and I formed together was unlikely, and yet, I think the unlikelihood is what made it so special. Without our losses, we would never have spoken. I would never have come to know her deeply genuine heart, her charismatic wit, and her contagious determination to grieve with joy. Among all the reasons I had to hate loss for its destruction, our friendship reminded me of all the reasons to be grateful.

This capacity for understanding is perhaps what makes the human heart so invincible. With empathy, we don't have to explain; we just feel together. Although this unspoken connection does not in any way soften the pain, it is the difference between breathing and deeply exhaling. It is the unsaid validation and the quiet awareness of what it means to lose someone.

Jen helped me realize that sharing experiences brings us one step closer to healing. And maybe healing isn't about lessening the pain at all; maybe it's more about seeing our blessings and choosing again and again to find joy. If we take this step, we might just be able to transform the ugliest part of grief into limitless potential.

GRIEVING IN A WAY THAT BRINGS YOU JOY

According to Jen, her mother Sue was "one of the most selfless, most considerate, most thoughtful people you've ever met."

As Jen told me about her childhood, I could see that her mother was the living embodiment of generosity. Not only was she a nurse with a desire to love and nurture everyone, but she was also an active member of the community. Sue spent her weekends volunteering at a community health organization that provided low-income families with medical screenings and checkups. Additionally, the Hale family owned a Christmas tree farm, and Sue was known for freely giving out Christmas trees during the holiday season.

Jen described her mother as "a serial gift giver." Sue worked hard to ensure every person felt loved and appreciated. "It's just who she was," Jen told me. "She did so much for the community, and everyone knew how thoughtful she was." Sue hardly went anywhere without a gift. When visiting her daughters in their adult years, she never arrived empty-handed; she always had some homemade cookies, laundry detergent, a card, any little present to remind her children how much she cared.

When reflecting on her childhood, Jen remembered one particular day in fifth grade. It was the end of the year, and

Jen had arrived at school with three shopping bags full of gifts for everyone: all her classmates, the staff, even a box of Good and Plenty candy for the gym teacher. "Looking back," Jen reflected, "she really thought hard about what each person wanted or what was a hobby that they liked. She just didn't want anyone to feel left out. She had to celebrate everybody by giving them gifts and letting them know that they were thought of."

During holidays, Sue was always passionate about transforming her house to match the spirit of the season. Jen recalled her mother's Winter Wonderlands and grand buffets of food for her family. Sue was always working tirelessly to make each experience a memorable one. "She did everything," Jen said. "As you can imagine, her impact on my life is very profound."

I couldn't help but simultaneously imagine my dad's holiday spirit each Christmas, as he would meticulously arrange our ceramic nativity set and then spend hours wrapping colored lights in the perfect position around our tree. I wondered if Sue Hale and my dad would have been friends.

The Hale family's life took a drastic, unexpected turn shortly after Christmas in December 2017, when Sue began experiencing debilitating headaches. As a result, she could not go to work and struggled to maintain her usual cheerful disposition.

Sue went to the doctor and received a diagnosis that chalked her headaches up to be "something of a virus," but Jen's older sister was a nurse and could sense it was something else. "This isn't you, Mom," she said, and took her mother to the emergency room.

After a CT scan, the doctors were suspicious of something potentially dangerous, so they decided to follow up with a more intensive MRI. There they received the news.

She had cancer in her brain. Lesions all over Sue's spine, lungs, and brain. Stage four lung cancer.

Jen told me about her inability to comprehend the diagnosis. Her mom had never smoked a day in her life, and the news seemed impossible. "I couldn't believe this was happening," she said. "Everyone was shocked by the diagnosis, but we were hopeful, even though it had spread. We followed the oncologist, and I remember him pulling me over to the computer, showing me my mother's scan, showing me her cancer and all of the different areas, and I could just see in his eyes that it was hopeless."

Sue was immediately put on a treatment plan with radiation and two rounds of chemotherapy. After the second round in early March, Sue's health had declined so rapidly that she could not even get out of bed to go to the hospital. She began receiving hospice treatment. In the short span of under two months, Jen had watched her lively, nurturing mother fall into a terminal illness. It was the foreshadowing of a nightmare, one Jen knew was coming but could not bring herself to fully accept.

But Jen also witnessed her mother fully embrace the unpredictability of life. I could hear her stifling tears as she recalled a memorable afternoon with her mother. Sue lovingly wiped a tear from her daughter's cheek and pushed a strand of hair behind her ear. "There is nothing like a mother's love," Jen said to me, and I had to agree. I only knew what it meant to lose my dad, but his death had molded my mom into a superhero.

Time and time again, I had seen her rise, giving and giving with everything in her heart. She had an endless amount of love inside her; although Jen couldn't see me, I was nodding my head in validation. Nothing on this Earth is like a mother's love.

As Sue's health began to deteriorate, Jen, her two sisters, and her father celebrated Easter together, trying to gather hope and suppress their fear of the future. "I knew she was going to die," Jen said. "I just had no idea when." I wondered what it was like to know death was near, selfishly wishing that sickness would have given me more time to prepare for my dad's passing—but then again, one can never prepare for such a loss.

Three short months after Sue's diagnosis, on April 25, 2018, Jen lost her mother. It was on her parents' thirty-seventh wedding anniversary. In three short months, the woman who had raised her and cultivated such kindness and generosity in hundreds of lives was gone. The devastation and shock were, of course, unbearable, a piercing culmination of emotions for the Hale family, but Jen felt her mom's timing was purposeful.

Jen eloquently delivered a touching eulogy at her mother's funeral. As she read me the words she wrote for that day, the tiny hairs stood up on my arm. "She died on her thirty-seventh wedding anniversary with my father, who she lovingly referred to as Huckleberry Finn in her final days," she wrote. "I believe she chose to leave on that day for a reason, because when you marry Huckleberry Finn, a grand adventure awaits. And when you die, another grand adventure awaits."

Jen told me about the hundreds of people present at Sue's funeral. Again, the same feeling rose inside me: that indescribable emotion of wonder and awe at the lives touched by a single person—a person who made you and loved you and raised you. That perspective would stay with me forever.

As Jen continued, she told me she was constantly talking about her loss. Whenever she thought about her mom, she felt compelled to share and keep her mother's memory alive. Her willingness to express the pain was all too familiar to me. Unlike my brothers who had struggled to talk about their grief, I too could not stop sharing my emotions. I had to write about it. I had to talk about it. I had to tell people, because the loss was deeply ingrained in me and the person I was becoming.

"The initial shock of her death rocked me to my core," Jen said. "My mother and I were very similar in a lot of ways; we were very similar creatures, which is why I was so affected by her death. I felt like I was taking it harder than everyone. After she died, I just couldn't get over it."

For Jen, support groups and therapy had a certain level of importance, but they also held their own aura of sadness that seemed to only intensify the pain. "I wanted to grieve in a way that reminded me of her, but not necessarily wallow in my emotions all the time," she said, "because I think there is a time for that, but I also think there is a time for you to unfortunately accept your new reality in your life. But you can do it in a way that brings you joy." Only then did I realize how much I needed to hear those words.

One day, a friend commented on how much Jen's laugh sounded like her mother's. Those simple words filled Jen with a sense of hope, and so only a few weeks later, she found herself as a certified laughter-yoga instructor. From the other end of the call, I was intrigued that this was even a practice. I wanted to know more, and I wanted to keep hearing her laugh; it felt like a portal to a tiny piece of Sue, a woman I desperately wish I could have met.

Jen told me these classes included laughter exercises and breathing techniques to combat stress and depression. After going to one session, she realized thirty minutes of voluntary laughter had profound effects on her mood. Now every week, Jen spends an hour of her time helping strangers work through these exercises. "Being able to share my laughter with other people to get them to laugh—not only is it a very healing process for me because I feel like I'm sharing my mother's joy and her laugh with other people, but also it helps them too."

As we continued to talk, I learned that Jen's search for positivity amid her grief was not just limited to this unique form of therapy. Shortly after her mom's death, Jen had visited a local farm, saw a woman feeding goats, and was immediately curious about the process. "I really felt strongly about taking care of something and wanting to nurture something," she recalled, after reaching out to the owner for more information. A few weeks later, she received a call that there was an opening to become a sheep feeder. I could hear the smile in her voice as she continued, "I didn't even know that was a thing," and I laughed in agreement.

In addition to laughter yoga, Jen spends a small portion of her Fridays interacting with and feeding sheep on the farm. As simple and maybe even strange as it may seem, her weekly experience has given her an outlet where she can channel her mom's nurturing character. "Who would have thought that those ten minutes of my day would bring me so much joy?" she said. "It's very strange, but it has helped me carry out the nurturing mother she was."

In the same way that Jen was looking to honor her mother's nurturing presence, I also felt compelled to carry on my dad's musical legacy. Together we were trying—trying to replicate those qualities within ourselves and live as a reflection of what our parents left behind.

Jen's quest for outlets to help her better navigate life without her mother didn't stop there. In December 2018, she collaborated with a friend to launch her own community group called "Have a Good Mourning." Unlike the other support groups that met in darkly lit church basements to rehash the painful details of loss, Jen's group was focused exactly on what a grieving heart needs—reasons to be happy.

I remember opening the blinds in my bedroom as she told me about her project. Maybe I was subconsciously letting the light in as Jen did. Staring out the window at the masses of students crossing the street, I could see the sun subtly shining through a few clouds. Most people had their heads down, eyes glued to their phones or the sidewalk. I thought about how each one was carrying their own story, their own journey, some maybe moving though a daily routine as monotonously as I was. The sky was gloomy, but a few promising rays found their way through my window and onto my bed. "The goal," Jen said, "was to show people that in spite of your loss, you can still enjoy yourself again."

Through this group, Jen and her friend work to get people into the community to do something fun and out of the ordinary. They go bowling, sing karaoke, and go on various outings around the city. "I wasn't trying to make light of death," she continued, "but show people that it's very transformative, while giving people the opportunity to smile and laugh again."

I watered the baby's breath on my windowsill. Jen was becoming a trusted confidant, a person who understood my pauses just as much as my words. I looked at the time stamp on my phone call; over an hour had passed, and still I wanted to know more about her story. Her conviction about the healing power of finding joy—it was contagious. As we elongated our goodbye, both unwilling to hang up, I realized grieving did not always mean drowning in sorrow and begging God for answers. Sometimes, it meant finding gratitude in the struggle and giving yourself room to grow. Purpose was a path we could create, a journey we had the power to change at any given moment.

Jen's story helped me recognize we can grieve in a way that brings us joy. Although the journey is by no means inherently joyful, we can learn to uncover small moments of peace and gratitude. The human heart is constructed for tragedy; even in the depths of loss, we still have a capacity for happiness. Grief and joy are meant to intertwine; after all, grieving is the sum of all the joy we have ever felt with someone we love. I never thought two things so seemingly incompatible could coexist in such a way, but Jen reminded me it is possible. It is possible to love again, to laugh again. It is possible to feel again, to feel the longing for the one you have lost and the gratitude for their existence all at once, because this is what grief does. This is what love does.

A MESSAGE IN MUSIC
"Because of You" by Gene Clark

CHAPTER 5

A HEART ON FIRE

I am continually amazed by life's ability to be equally beautiful and devastating.

—JUNE 19, 2018, DAD'S FIRST BIRTHDAY IN HEAVEN

It is strange how, when someone dies, we can see their best qualities in almost perfect light, a holistic memory of those precious moments we often failed to see when they were here. For so long, I blamed myself for these missed moments. I blamed myself for all the times I should have said "I love you" and could have thanked him for everything before it was too late.

One afternoon, while making a scrapbook for Mother's Day, I went rummaging through a few plastic bins in my mom's room. The bins were overflowing with random bills, crumpled computer paper, and messy notepads; feeling a bit defeated, I kept digging, hoping I could find a piece of my dad's existence to put in the scrapbook for her. As I reached the bottom of one box, I could see his handwriting on chaotic to-do lists and scraps of soccer coaching drills. These things had been so insignificant at one time, but now, they were invaluable archives of his life.

Surrounded by piles of paper, I took out the final sheet. It read: Paul's Goals . . . March 3, 1997. Underneath the title was a list of fifty goals—a (very ambitious) bucket list. I did the math. He had written it at twenty-six years old. I shoved the rest of the papers to the side and sat down to read. Finding treasures like this list that I didn't know existed were, much like my dad, always full of surprises.

Paul's Goals...3/3/97
1. Write Books
2. Marry Jill and have a big family
3. Get my teaching certificate
4. Get my Masters
5. Get a Ph.D.
6. Skydive
7. Hang Glide
8. Weigh 170lbs
9. Play in a band, record a CD
10. Adopt a child
11. Travel to Italy, France, Africa, Hawaii, Brazil.
12. Get my Pilot's License
13. Learn how to do a back flip
14. Help Abused Children
15. Meet Mother Theresa, Pele, the Pope, Reggie White
16. Compete in a Triathalon
17. Learn to Rock Climb
18. Learn how to rollerblade
19. Coach College Soccer
20. Help homeless, poor, etc.
21. Go to a Packer Game @ Lambeau
22. Learn to Kayak
23. Own a Ferrari
24. Be able to Slam Dunk
25. Run the 40 in under 4.8sec
26. Run in a Marathon
27. Take Guitar, Drum, Piano, Voice Lessons until I'm good at them
28. Travel to a third world country to help the unfortunate
29. Work against Racism, Prejudice, and Hate
30. Work for Peace and Justice
31. Work / Write for a Newspaper
32. Host my own talk show
33. Drive a Stock Car
34. Get in the Guiness Book of World Records
35. Write a Play and / or Screenplay
36. Own a Plane
37. Own a boat
38. Build a Dream home w/ landing strip, pool, observatory, library & field on a lake
39. Own a modest home in the Rockies, Sierras or overlooking the Ocean
40. Learn Martial Arts
41. Become a gormet chef
42. Become a great humanitarian
43. Shine a light so that all will know that God is visible in my life through my words, thoughts, and actions
44. Work to end Abortion
45. Get up early every morning
46. Watch many Sunrises
47. Watch a Sunset
48. Exercise every day for the rest of my life
49. Spread the Word of God
50. Make a huge difference in the World

"A Life isn't significant exect for it's impact on other's lives..."   Jackie Robinson

1) Write books

He was always a writer at heart, and I knew that, with more time, he could have written a bestseller—maybe an espionage thriller or a passionate love story.

2) Marry Jill and have a big family

This one was highlighted in blue. Alleviating some of the heartache with an exhale, I smiled. He had accomplished his greatest goal. We were the big family.

As I continued to read, the goals became loftier and even laughable.

Things like: Build a dream home with a landing strip, pool, observatory, library, and field on a lake brought my smile to a laugh, in awe of this list that so perfectly captured his fearless character.

Other goals on the list were indicative of his giving nature.

14) Help abused children

20) Help the homeless

28) Travel to a third-world country to help the unfortunate

29) Work against racism, prejudice, and hate

And then the one that tightened my stomach into a knot:

43) Shine a light so that all will know that God is visible in my life through my thoughts, words, and actions

At the very bottom of the list, he had typed a quote by Jackie Robinson:

"A life isn't significant except for its impact on other's lives . . ."

This line embodied his entire approach to life. My dad was a man who lived to leave a lasting imprint on everyone.

Sitting there for a few minutes, I took in that piece of paper. I imagined my dad as a twenty-six-year-old, hunched over a massively thick Macintosh computer, documenting his dreams for the years to come. He was completely unaware his life would end almost exactly two decades later, and his daughter would stumble across this list only two months after that. He did not think anyone would ever see the list, and there I was, clutching the paper to my chest, grateful and devastated by the opportunity to hold his dreams in my hands.

I photocopied the list and taped it to my wall. I was determined to accomplish those things left un-highlighted. I could write a book. I could skydive. I could travel to Europe and learn to play guitar and record a CD. At one time, I would have thought I had my whole life ahead of me to accomplish these things, but I had learned you never have enough time, and when you have the chance to do something, do it.

I couldn't stop thinking about his forty-third goal. Unknowingly, he had always been a shining exemplar of God's light. That's just who he was. As I climbed into bed each night with his bucket list hanging on my wall, I thought about how he was the definition of what it meant to be kind. My dad's entire life was fueled by the desire to help anyone and everyone. Although he always exhibited this quality, I didn't fully recognize its magnitude until he was gone.

Now, I can see that every action was an intention to give. After a snowstorm, he was always the first one outside in the cold, snow-blowing and shoveling everyone's lawn and every sidewalk in the neighborhood. On his way home from work in the winter, he sometimes stopped to offer strangers rides so they wouldn't have to wait in freezing temperatures for the bus. This generosity of course terrified my mom for safety reasons, but he insisted it was the right thing to do.

On Father's Day, my dad would spend a solid hour or so on the couch, sifting through his contacts and texting every single father in his phone a personalized, heartfelt message. On Thanksgiving, Christmas, and Easter, he did the same. I never understood why he took the time to do so, but now I get it: for him, thinking about people was never a bullet point on a to-do list or a social obligation, but a natural instinct that fueled his life.

With my brothers and me, he practiced these same principles of generosity. He was the type of father who stayed up all night to make our Halloween costumes or build my brothers a pinewood derby car more legendary than the year before.

If we needed help with homework, he sat with us and flipped through flashcards until we understood the material. If we were having a sleepover, he went to the store and returned with soda, candy, ice cream, and popcorn. If one of us was sick, the remedy included everything under the sun: a bowl of soup, endless cough drops, nasal spray, tissues, comfy pillows, and Flamin' Hot Cheetos for decongestion.

I specifically remember one night in third grade, when I had procrastinated starting an assignment about our ancestry. The project involved using a large, traditional clothespin (with a rounded tip) to make a person who represented our heritage. I had lost the clothespin, and even after scouring the entire house, I could not find it. By midnight, my perfectionist tendencies had taken over and I was an anxious, dramatic ten-year-old, pitiably sobbing that I would get a bad grade. My dad convinced me to go to bed, although I was distressed about arriving to social studies class empty-handed.

When I woke up the next morning, the clothespin was sitting on the table. It had a convincing face, complete with a paper alpine hat and felt lederhosen. My dad had stayed up the entire night, found the clothespin buried in a junk drawer, and finished my project to perfection while I slept. It was just a clothespin and just a third-grade project, but I think that's the reason I remember it so well. He always sacrificed so much, even for the smallest thing, if he knew it mattered to someone.

ACTS OF KINDNESS

What would have been my dad's forty-seventh birthday felt like a convergence of unexpected paradoxes. I didn't realize how disorienting it would be to celebrate a milestone so centered around the idea of life. It almost felt wrong. For me, acknowledging the day was just a startling reminder to count another year of his life that could have been. It was an obligatory recognition of all the years ahead of us, years where we could only imagine what it would be like to see my dad age. I'd never see his black hair slowly peppered by gray, never watch him bounce my kids on his knee to tell them a story.

Among all the painful days I knew I would have to endure, this one by far felt the most incongruous.

Although I was resistant to celebrating this first birthday without him, my mom was insistent on acknowledging it. We made plans to buy some balloons for his grave, sing "Happy Birthday," and then watch a World Cup game at a local sports bar. So we all picked out some decorations and drove to the cemetery. As I stood at the foot of the dirt mound with a bouquet of yellow roses in hand, I couldn't help but wonder what birthdays were like somewhere eternal.

The spot where he was buried was still blanketed in pieces of straw, the surface untouched, my wounds fresh. We attempted to sing a lively "Happy Birthday," starting off strong before our voices tanked into a mopey, unfinished melody. We tried again. My mom threw some rose petals into the air and we fixed the balloons onto a pinwheel; it felt better, but still weird, considering we were all staring at the grass, wondering why three months without him felt like a lifetime.

* * *

When we got to the restaurant, my mom told us about a book she had a read a few weeks prior about something called "The Kindness Project." The book traced the story of Joanne Cacciatore, a woman who had a stillborn daughter and then decided to channel her grief into random acts of kindness. Joanne's healing journey began when she bought a bunch of toys for underprivileged kids through a local charity with the money she would have used to buy her daughter's Christmas presents. This generosity quickly became habit. Joanne began making acts of kindness a daily practice toward strangers by searching for opportunities to make their day.[8]

In her experience discovering the power of giving, Joanne wrote, "While these good deeds do not eradicate grief, nor should they do so, they provide a means through which the

---

8   Joanna Cacciatore, *Bearing the Unbearable: Love, Loss, and the Heartbreaking Path of Grief.* Wisdom Publications. 2017.

mourner can redirect painful emotions into feelings of love and compassion and hope." In the years following her daughter's death, Joanne developed a platform for grieving people by encouraging them to do good deeds in memory of someone. She said that leaving behind a small notecard with the name of a loved one allows people to work toward healing.[9]

After reading the book, my mom was inspired to carry out Joanne's mission. I knew she was desperately searching for ways to keep my dad's memory alive, and the act of cultivating generosity from our empty world was exactly what she needed. So when we walked into the restaurant and slid into a corner booth, she was eager to give.

A middle-aged man was sitting a few feet away from us, eating alone and working from his laptop. At the end of our meal, my mom went to the register, asked for his receipt, and paid for his meal. Underneath the bill, at the bottom, she wrote, In memory of the best dad ever! punctuated with a tiny smiley face. We watched as the man received his bill and scanned the room, confused. He had no idea it was us.

We stole glances in his direction, sneaking smiles at each other, attempting not to blow our cover. It felt so good. I didn't even know we had anything left in our hearts to give away, but we did; an infinite amount of love was inside each of us, and sharing it felt electric. When the man stood up and slung his backpack over his shoulder, he turned to reveal a tattoo of a giant, winding music staff on his bicep. The five of us were stunned. We sat back in our seats and exhaled in a mix of shock, wonder, and gratitude.

---

9   Cacciatore, Joanne. *Bearing the Unbearable: Love, Loss,
     and the Heartbreaking Path of Grief.*

There are many things I attribute to coincidences, but I'd like to think this moment wasn't one of them. The timing, the connection, the beauty born from a simple and random act of kindness—it was all too comforting to be something of an accidental nature. In the months following that day, my family decided that giving was a necessary part of the journey. My Aunt Ann designed small, brightly colored notecards that said:

Have a Great Day!—inspired by Paul Sanchez's life—His heart was full and always kind. We hope this made you smile.

I started carrying these around in my wallet. Whenever I found myself feeling most alone, I tried to remind myself to give. Sometimes it was buying coffee for the person in line behind me, sometimes it was sending a handwritten letter. These small acts by no means erased my constant twinges of grief, but they made me feel closer to my dad. Amid all the triggers of my personal tragedy, giving reminded me—I was still capable of good.

A HEART ON FIRE

As we made ourselves comfortable in our living room, waiting patiently to open presents, my mom handed each of us a small brown bag. It was the second Christmas without him, and the concept of almost two years felt unfeasible.

Prefacing the gift, she told us about a book she read on her silent retreat: *Hearts on Fire.* It was a collection of Jesuit prayers, a book my dad had also read on the same retreat a decade earlier. He brought the book home with him, where it remained on his nightstand for years. The pages were folded and ruffled from use, and the front cover still had a mysterious sticker residue in the corner.

My mom told us about her experience of sitting in the chapel, feeling his presence come over her. When she removed a copy of *Hearts on Fire* from the bookshelf, she read the sticker in bold print: *Please do not bring this book out of the chapel. You can buy them in the gift shop.*

Yes, my dad stole the book.

All irony aside, the book meant something to him. The Jesuit order's entire mission was focused on being "men and women for others," a selfless philosophy that my dad carried throughout his entire life. Passionate to share his gifts, whether that meant a hug, a ride, a thoughtful text, or the grand gesture of finding a clothespin at 4 a.m., he never let this inner flame die.

My brothers and I removed the little red paperback from the tissue paper. I traced the soft cover and the spine, turning it over in my hands. "Your dad had a heart on fire," my mom said.

With his fervent spirit and hunger for life, kindness, and joy, my dad had unknowingly illuminated a path for us to follow. He had given us gifts that taught us how to give. With a small flame of that fire igniting inside me, I could feel it gradually growing, burning into a bright, unstoppable blaze.

A MESSAGE IN MUSIC
"Diamonds Made From Rain" by Eric Clapton

CHAPTER 6

THE MAGICIAN

———

I am trying to remind myself that with every breath we draw,
we can inhale your very presence.

—JUNE 19, 2019, A LETTER TO MY FATHER

My dad always carried a pack of playing cards, ready to shuffle them at any given moment for a magic trick. There was a full deck in every room of the house, only a fingertip's reach from wherever he was sitting. He was constantly toying with them, leaving a wake of misplaced kings and queens wherever he went.

While driving, lying in bed, or even sitting at a restaurant table, he would twirl a card or two between his fingers before throwing it upwards and gracefully vanishing it from sight. In one swift gesture, he would reach behind my ear to extract a card and say, "Ha! How'd that get there?" He often sat at his desk outside my bedroom for hours on end, just shuffling his precious cards while he worked; the sound never failed to lull me to sleep.

It seemed that in every place my dad had been, there was a trail of his little magic tricks. My family usually reprimanded him for his haphazardly thrown cards. I found them every-where: in the car glove compartment, under my bed, book-marked in magazines, a few wedged between two living room couch cushions. Our house became a growing archive of the decades my dad had spent fascinated with entertainment magic.

As a little girl, I always overflowed with pride to introduce my dad as a "magician." His extensive knowledge of magic tricks was not limited to his sleight of hand. Inside dozens of plastic bins, he had gimmicks of all sorts: colorful handker-chiefs, inflatable magic wands, fake cigarettes that emitted a convincing flame for the sake of illusion. Magic was just a hobby, but my dad believed doing anything without full-blown effort was not worth doing at all.

In first grade, when the rotation landed on me to be the "Star of the Week," I naturally chose him to be my guest. Most of my classmates brought in their parents, who usually read a story or baked cookies for the class, but I knew my guest was going to be different than anyone they had seen before.

My dad wholeheartedly embraced the role. He arrived wearing a black top hat, with a suitcase and giant inflatable wand to play the part. Everyone huddled together on the carpet, a classroom of crisscross-applesauce and inquisitive eyes. He started by asking for a few volunteers, and twenty-five hands shot in the air.

After selecting two of my classmates to stand up, my dad's performance started with the iconic coloring book stunt. He handed one of them the inflatable wand and then flipped through the pages of a blank coloring book.

"I think this could use some color," he playfully mused, rubbing his stubbled chin. "Here." He gestured to the girl next to him. "Why don't you give it a try?"

She hesitantly tapped the book with her wand.

"C'mon, like you mean it!" he teased, playfully grabbing her wrist and demonstrating how to put a spell on the book. With her tiny arm still in hand, he began whacking himself on the head with the wand.

"Hey! Stop hitting me!" The room of tiny first-graders erupted in laughter. The girl giggled and purposely tapped the top of his head again, then the book in his hands. When he opened it and shuffled through the pages, one of the drawings was filled with color.

The class was mesmerized. I continued to watch with pride as the cadence of audible "ooh's" and "aah's" filled the classroom. Next came his three shells: the hallmark trick of all magicians involving three plastic walnut halves and one rubber pea. He swiftly maneuvered the shells around his black coin pad, mixing them up to mislead the location of the pea. When his selected volunteers guessed the wrong shell, he lifted all three to reveal an empty table, then reached behind one of my classmate's ears and materialized a rubber pea.

The class loved my dad. He continued his performance by pretending to sneeze and producing a seemingly endless color handkerchief from his nose. A few kids yelled, "How'd you do that?" He smirked, proud that his efforts were fascinating their youthful minds. "A magician never reveals his secrets," he taunted.

To make sure everyone had a chance to volunteer, my dad withdrew his levitating sphere, the disappearing bottle, and the giant spiral illusion on a poster board. He continued to astonish the room of spell-bound first-graders, calling on every student until they were convinced he was a wizard.

I now realize that magic was not just an entertaining hobby for my dad; it was a way he connected with people. His magic tricks facilitated small talk at restaurants, impressed nieces and nephews, and fascinated children on the playground during recess duty. Whenever I brought a new friend to the house, my dad insisted they watch a card trick. When there was a block party or a family function, he was determined to capture the interest of someone, through a coin appearing in their ear or a bottle vanishing before their eyes. This little bit of mystery attracted so much intrigue and happiness, enchanting minds of every age.

At one time, the sound of shuffling cards was just noise. Now I cannot hear the whirring cards without thinking of the man who breathed years of magic into my childhood.

NOSTALGIA

I sat on the edge of my bed, my right arm limply draped over my guitar, my eyes staring blankly at the wall in front of me. I lazily fumbled through the few chords I knew. An F, a C, a mediocre G. My mind was elsewhere, immersed in a time and place where I did not yet exist. I closed my eyes and could see my parents, in 1991, nineteen years old and madly in love. A few words found their way to the surface of my mind.

The queen of hearts
She was the start
A life of love and hope

I leaned back into the headboard and abruptly started to cry. I wondered: was it possible to be nostalgic for an era you never lived? I scribbled a few more words into my journal.

I took her hand
She took my name
And watched our children grow

As I tried to piece my thoughts together into something that resembled lyrics, a clear metaphor began to emerge. It had only been a few months since my dad died, and I was craving a way to channel my pain. I was desperately searching for something that could capture him, me, the story of his life, and the emptiness eating away at me from the inside out. I opened the Voice Memos app on my phone, recorded that first verse, and felt oddly satisfied with the melody.

In some ways, writing felt like exhaling. I had hardly taken time to let my new reality sink in, but in my attempts to craft a second verse, I suddenly felt more in tune with myself than I had in a long time. I wrote a little more.

A waiting room, gone too soon
A king's unfinished reign
A heart as numb as broken drums
Magic running through our veins

I envisioned my entire family—all my aunts, uncles, grandparents, cousins, my brothers and my mom—crowded into that tiny waiting room with our heads hanging low in disbelief. And then all at once, it came to me. Dropping my phone in shock and watching it shatter. My uncle crying. Sitting on a stool and holding my dad's calloused hand. My brother running out of the room. Prayers. Hugs. Frantic phone calls. The smell of sweat and tears, the murmur of doors opening and hearts breaking.

I found myself paralyzed by this image as if I had never lived it in the first place. But somehow, I was simultaneously graced by an almost magical image of his love coursing through our veins that day we lost him. I could see my dad soaring on his way to somewhere, wherever that was, wearing his contagious, million-watt smile. I strummed a few chords, trying to convince myself I was somewhat capable of playing an instrument. As the words came out, they felt . . . right.

The magician's on his way
Throwing down an ace of spades
He's got music in his blood
I see the magic in his love
Never ever going away

After reading over my thoughts, I felt lighter. My dad had been a both a phenomenal musician and avid magician, and I wanted to weave these elements into a sort of song that was both nostalgic and hopeful—a song of longing for what once was and what was yet to come. Since I was little, I had always made up songs on the spot, but this time, doing so felt more necessary than ever before. The content was painfully real.

As a matter of fact, this was the first "real" song I had ever written, and I had picked up the guitar only a few months earlier, attempting to emulate my dad's love of music. As I began to fill the pages of my journal with this imagery of my dad on his way to Heaven, I could not believe how cathartic it felt. I found it strange to outline the past few weeks of my life in a few honest phrases—vulnerable pieces of my heart that was still so numb.

Whenever the grief was overpowering, my thoughts always had a home on paper. My perpetual quest to find the right words in the English language always left me sleepless, dumping my feelings into a journal at odd hours of the night. Writing was merely a form of catharsis, but this new collection of feeling could not be contained by any words at all. Attempting and always failing to string together sentences, I realized some languages are better felt than spoken.

A MESSAGE IN MUSIC
"Some Day Soon" by Alexi Murdoch

CHAPTER 7

THE WEIGHT OF WINTER

——

I sit at your grave and wonder what eternal life feels like, for this one without you feels infinite.

—AUGUST 9, 2018, A LETTER TO MY FATHER

The ballroom was mostly empty, with hotel staff beginning to remove tablecloths and stack chairs. I wasn't ready to leave. The night had been quintessential in every way: chocolate cheesecake, classic jams, dance circles with dads attempting to do the worm. I wiped the sweat from my forehead and tried to catch my breath; Whitney Houston's lyrics had all the diehard dancers begging for another song, and my dad and I were leading the chant for an encore.

At my high school, the Father-Daughter Dance was always the most iconic dance of the year, and I couldn't seem to accept this night as my last one. Moments from the previous three hours surfaced in my mind in images: slipping my heels off and running barefoot on the cold wood floor, freeing my hair from its ponytail, strumming the air guitar next to my dad in a coordinated-but-not-coordinated telepathic performance. Surrounded by my best friends and their dads, we had belted every song, with a mix of nostalgia, sweat, and adrenaline. Bringing myself back to the present moment, I reached down to dust off the balls of my feet, saw that my blackened heels were a lost cause, and dragged my dad toward the front of the stage.

As the dance floor emptied, a soothing string of piano chords filled the room—the signal of a slow song. My dad took my hand in his, pulled me close, and smiled. I could still smell his aftershave.

"I'll give you five dollars if you can tell me who this is." It was a challenge that my brothers and I were used to hearing. If we could identify the greatest songs of his time, he considered his parenting a success.

I scrunched up my face, wracking my brain for the answer. A light drum rhythm and the rich sound of a melodica enveloped the room. In a matter of seconds, my quiz time was up. "Uh, I don't know," I shrugged, disappointed in myself.

"Lionel Richie!" My dad leaned in, poking my shoulder, overly eager to reveal the answer. I took a mental note and pressed my head to his chest. I easily could have fallen asleep like that, with my ear against his heart and his thumb gently stroking mine. My eyes felt heavy, closing over the colorful blur of DJ lights and swaying bodies.

"Hey, guess what?" he whispered, but I already knew what he was going to say. I turned my face toward him, the stubble on his chin grazing my forehead.

"What?"

"I love you." I felt a light kiss at the top of my head. Lionel Richie's "Easy" echoed through the ballroom, a song that would entwine with that moment forever. I was on the brink of tears; I just felt so old. Three years earlier, I had been standing in a similar spot as an awkward freshman, naively abandoning him on the dance floor to go take pictures with my friends. Two years earlier, he had been freshly out of heart surgery, spending most of his time at the table trying to catch his breath. One year ago, we stood together before the live band, mesmerized by the lead singer's talent and voice range. "You have to have a live band at your wedding," he always said. "You have to."

And now, graduation was a few months away. Senior year was filled with endings, and this dance was the first of many lasts.

As we box-stepped around our corner of the dance floor, I felt small in his arms, in the same way I had as a little girl. Somehow, the years of my life had passed quickly, and this new, unknown chapter was approaching even more quickly. Closing my eyes, I allowed myself to fall into the final minute of the song and relish the moment before it was just a memory.

"I love you too." My voice was a childish whisper.

Sweat beaded his forehead and hairline—a testament to all his passionate dance moves of the night: the shopping cart, the sprinkler, a convincing disco and imaginary drum solo for every song.

"You look just like your mother," he whispered, pushing my hair out of my face. The concluding notes of the song rang out, and I melted into his hug. We lingered for a few extra seconds as the dance floor cleared and the quiet murmur of conversation returned. Had I known it would be the last time I would ever dance with him, I would have hung on forever.

AN IMPENDING HOLIDAY

The weight of Christmas approaching brought more obsta-cles than I expected. We had already survived several of those dreaded firsts, but the onset of December bore a different type of heaviness. As if the persistent holiday cheer was not enough, the falling snow served as another reminder that the seasons were changing; time was passing, and in the most unforgiving way.

When I came home for winter break, visiting my dad's grave felt suffocating. All the snow blanketing his resting place seemed like a visual representation of the growing space between us. We were a universe apart, and still, life continued to layer on more burdens. Wisconsin winters are an elongated spell of frigid days and unrelenting darkness, but I knew this time I could not blame the cold. The lack of light in my world was something much stronger and more permanent, and this was a valley I could not avoid.

I spent most of December in a daze between denial and distraction. I did not want to accept another month—nine whole months—without my dad. My days were consumed by half-hearted attempts to study for finals and long, depressive naps that left me a hopeless insomniac by nighttime. I found it hard to care.

Simultaneously, December was punctuated by small moments of anticipation. For eight months, the thought of getting a tattoo had remained a passive notion in the back of my mind. Before his death, I never understood the desire for something so permanent and irreversible, but now I almost needed it. If the pain was permanent, I wanted a lasting rep-resentation of that pain. If my heart was going to ache like this forever, I deserved a visual battle wound.

A few words from a creative English paper I wrote in high school, which had compared tattoos to scars, continued to echo in the back of my head:

The similarities between tattoos and scars transcend all physical differences and prove that these markings are much more than mere imprints or healed wounds on the body. Each tattoo embodies a unique story, and every scar represents a profound experience. Despite the differences between these two indelible markings, tattoos and scars exhibit the same value beneath their surface; they both generate individuality and encourage a search beyond the body's exterior into the deepest corners of the human mind and soul.

No one ever tells you that grief makes you question your every choice; suddenly, your every thought becomes a constant pursuit to honor the one you have lost and to make them proud. My dad hated tattoos—call it paternal instincts or just traditional values, but either way, I could not help overthinking what he might say if he were here. For months, I ruminated on the possibilities, weighing my overpowering grief against the what if's and the "maybe's.

I went with my gut. One Friday, after my last final exam, my Aunt Staci and my mom drove me to Green Bay, Wisconsin, to see a renowned artist who designed tattoos for the Green Bay Packers. The entire ride there, I studied the skin on my arm, a blank canvas soon to be covered with a lifelong reminder of all I had lost.

I took a deep breath and scooted onto a reclining leather chair, while the owner, Rick, gently brushed my arm with an antiseptic wipe. Inhaling anxiously and breathing in my surroundings, I reached for Aunt Staci's hand. With my forearm sweating against the leather, I thought, This is it—no going back now.

Wincing as the needle touched my wrist, I peeked to see the outline of my very first tattoo forming on my skin: a tiny black pair of beamed eighth notes.

Turning my wrist in all directions under the fluorescent studio lights, I observed the ink as it settled on my skin. Forever imprinted on my body was a reminder of the man who brought music into my life. I could always look at my wrist and remember everything he left behind, the songs that shaped me and maybe even saved me.

It was a minimalistic tattoo, easily hidden with a watch or a sweater, but I think that's why it embodied him so well. For a man who somehow made grand gestures in such a humble and quiet way, I didn't need an extravagant reminder. His imprint on me was indelible, and that was what mattered.

I turned sideways on the plastic recliner and braced myself for a second tattoo.

Rick cleaned my side while I continued to squeeze Aunt Staci's hand. During my senior year retreat, parents had been encouraged to write their kids letters. The one I received from my dad became the last letter he ever wrote to me. I had leaned against a wall in a darkly lit room, unfolded the computer paper, and cried as I read. His words to me were unparalleled:

You are so incredibly talented and are never afraid to show how gifted you are. Always be compassionate throughout your life and let your light shine for everyone to see. Ask the Lord to come into your life and guide you in all ways closer to him. The best way to grow closer is to invite him into your life every day. Spend time praying, talking, and most importantly, listening to him speaking to your heart. Remember, your faith is the most special gift of God calling you to fall deeper in love with him. Fall deeper in love with God and grow in your faith.

At the bottom, in his impeccable handwriting:

Love, Dad

Although I had not talked to God in a long time, I clung to my dad's words about faith. Wasn't this just the simplified version of what it meant to live? To share our gifts and show compassion? It seemed like the most digestible answer to me. All my life, my dad's wisdom had been a driving force behind most of my decisions. There was something so compelling about his philosophy on the world, and I always took his advice as the truth. If anything, his death had taught me that life wasn't supposed to be measured in things like numbers or time or success. The only thing worth measuring, it seemed, was love.

As Rick traced the first letter of my dad's signature onto my rib cage, I squeezed Aunt Staci's hand again until it turned white. I could feel the long, calligraphic sweeping of the L, a delicate o, his gentle v and tiny e. I grimaced while the needle pierced my skin. A comma, then the D, a, d. When I stood up to look in the mirror, I could not believe how elegant it looked. In his beautiful cursive, the words darkened on my skin, slightly red and swollen around the edges. I ran my finger over the ink, grimacing and smiling and crying in the same breath. There it was in writing, on me, forever: a reminder to always live with love.

THE LITTLE ANGEL

One week before Christmas, my family group chat buzzed with a text from my Uncle Andy; there had been a devastating complication with my Aunt Leslie's pregnancy. After receiving an ultrasound for their fifteen-week appointment, the doctor told them their baby had no heartbeat.

My aunt's pregnancy had felt like a miracle for our family, a hopeful life blossoming in the face of overwhelming grief. When I first heard they were expecting, a renewed sense of hope had begun to form inside me. However, the news of my cousin left me with complete distrust in the world.

The following day, I arrived at their house to babysit my cousins while they went to the hospital. Hugging my aunt, I swallowed my sobs before they left to induce delivery of their stillborn son. I wondered how one could endure a milestone like this one, where joy in all capacities was tarnished by death.

While sifting through Legos and trying to distract myself, my four-year-old cousin, RJ, looked up from his building blocks and abruptly declared, "The baby is with God." I looked at him, unsure of what to say and partly convinced I'd misheard him. Kids had a miraculous way of stating life's truths in the most innocent and thought-provoking ways.

"Yeah, you're right," I said, speaking more to myself than RJ. He already knew what I could not accept.

"He's with Uncle Paul," RJ declared matter-of-factly, fixing a yellow Lego onto a blue one.

I stared into the eyes of this child, deprived of words, blinking back tears. The anger had completely incapacitated me from thinking about Heaven. I didn't know what else to say except another quiet "Yeah, you're right." I repeated these words to myself as I assembled a miniature white picket fence around a house, thinking about how a four-year-old was telling me everything I needed to hear.

When I drove home that night, I battled with my thoughts for an hour before sitting in my driveway and collapsing into tears. I never met my new little cousin and never would.

They had named him Stephen Anthony, using the same middle name as my dad. No one seemed to ever talk about this type of loss, the kind that stole life before it even began. Turning up Kenny Chesney's "Who You'd Be Today," I sorted through my thoughts and welcomed the way my emotions consumed me.

* * *

I had learned life was guaranteed to bring you to your knees, but I had not realized it brings you to your knees time and time again. Tragedy strikes at any given moment, at all stages of life. That day generated a curiosity in me about what it must be like for birth and death to collide so intimately. I knew I would never see my dad grow old, but what happens when you lose the opportunity to watch someone grow up? How do people carry on when death steals an entire childhood?

The Kroll family was a long-time friend of my family ever since I was little, and their experience served as proof that in every loss, we can find hope. I reached out to Ann Kroll, interested to know more about her story. As we sipped coffee together one afternoon, I found myself graced by her positivity. She told me about her emotions, her changed perspective, and her empowering faith in God.

As I sat across the table, I couldn't help but lean closer, drawing toward her and her inspirational outlook on the world. Hanging on to her every word, I listened intently, in awe of the way grief strengthens the human soul.

THE LITTLE FLOWER

In 2004, Michael and Ann Kroll were ecstatic about expecting their second child. Their son Caleb was almost three years old, and they were proud parents, excited to give him a sibling. However, when the couple went in for their twenty-week appointment, the doctor detected a complication through the ultrasound. Their baby was going to be born with anencephaly, a rare birth defect that involves an absence of a major part of the skull and scalp. Ann described to me how shaken they were, but with a strong faith and optimistic attitude, they had hope for their child. Their doctor had offered termination of the pregnancy. I could see the frustration still present in her eyes as she said, "It wasn't an option for us to terminate. We were, of course, going to carry her to term. We never questioned God as to why or why us. We accepted God's plan with grace."

On May 3, 2005, while working on an origami project with one of her art students, Ann went into labor. It was six weeks before her due date, and despite plans for induction, she rushed to the hospital for delivery, praying for a miraculous outcome. She understood that the statistics for children born with anencephaly were not promising; however, she and her husband desperately hoped to meet their daughter. "Most people terminate their babies with this condition and never get to meet their child," she told me. "We prayed for a miracle, but we also prayed that we could at least meet her alive.

After several hours, Ann gave birth to a baby girl. "The miracle was answered in that she was born alive," she said. They named her Rosalyn Ann and instantly baptized her. Ann withdrew a laminated card with a picture of her daughter, bordered in light pink. I turned the card over in my hand and read the last verse of the song "The Rose."

Cupping my coffee between two hands, I asked Ann about the origin of their daughter's name. She told me that "Rosalyn" had been inspired by St. Therese of Lisieux, who is known as "The Little Way" and "The Little Flower." "Everyone that met her was forever changed," Ann said. Because her little life had impacted people so much, Ann and Michael decided to call their newborn "Baby Rose."

"She lived for about an hour," Ann said to me, and I shifted my weight in the chair. One hour of life seemed so incomprehensible to me. How was it possible that one's first and final breath could be a mere sixty minutes apart?

Ann continued by telling me that aside from her missing skull cap, Baby Rose had been born healthy and fully formed. It had been nearly fourteen years, but the emotions from that day were still evidently palpable as she described them, "You feel like a semi just blew you over. Your mind races and it's so hard to cope with."

However, in the wake of such profound loss, Ann and Michael found the strength to recognize beauty. "As hard as it was," she said, "we were also given a gift. Everyone that met her was changed. She is a saint to us. We pray to her for strength and we look forward to meeting her again."

More questions began to surface inside me as I listened to this woman, one who was captivatingly faithful despite her loss. I thought about all the gifts I had seen in my own life after my dad's passing: the people, the kindness, the generosity—almost too many blessings to count. I would have, of course, given anything in a heartbeat if it meant getting my dad back. However, Ann made it so beautifully obvious that without our losses, we wouldn't have been sitting together sipping coffee and staring out the window. I might have never questioned my faith, never considered its powerful nature as she sat before me, living proof that God works in mysterious ways.

Ann described to me her daughter's memorial, where they scattered roses and prayed through the emptiness. She told me about how they met several other people who had also lost infants.

She told me about her following pregnancies, which included multiple miscarriages. When anyone asks her how many kids they have, she always says, "Six, but four on earth."

There is not a day that goes by where Ann, Michael, and their family do not think of Baby Rose. "You really don't get over it," Ann said as I nodded my head in agreement. "You just learn to live with it. And it does get a little bit easier, but you never forget." The pangs of never seeing their daughter grow up have come with endless challenges, but they have also blossomed into a passionate, intimate faith with God. Ann wears her grief like a shining battle wound and does not hesitate to share her story. Every text she sent to me ended with a rose emoji; their precious daughter remains so intimately connected with every aspect of their life.

As Ann and I hugged goodbye that day, I thought about how powerful perspective was. Here she was, fourteen years later, still able to articulate her experience as if it were yesterday. And yet, it was the way she told her story that brought me to tears, even happy tears. For the first time in a while, I was overcome with nothing but gratitude. Grief is a rollercoaster, a wreckage, an endless storm, the sum of all the emptiness we feel in the wake of a person's absence—but it is also the sum of all our love.

I remembered a quote I had once seen: "Grief, I've learned, is really just love. It's all the love you want to give but cannot. All that unspent love gathers up in the corners of your eyes, the lump in your throat, and that hollow part in your chest. Grief is just love with no place to go."[10]

On the surface, the two experiences seemed like polar opposites; after all, grief is pain, and love is an antidote to pain, right? But with Ann's story, I was learning that grief and love are inseparable because they are more or less the same. Love after loss feels intransitive; it is an accumulation of memories, longing, and attachment to someone we can no longer see.

Grief is a consequence of the risk we took for loving someone, but I like to think that the risk is worth it—that paying the price means we loved deeply and that our loss was of immense value. The capacity for loving guarantees

---

10 "Jamie Anderson Quotes," Goodreads, Jamie Anderson, accessed February 1, 2020.

pain, and the two bleed together to remind us that heartbreak is just our love in pieces, fragments that we hold close and share with others who understand. Fragments that inspire us to carry on, making us better, stronger, wiser. Grief, in its every form, is love, and on that day, I had never been more certain.

A MESSAGE IN MUSIC
"Little Flower" by Peter Bradley Adams, ALIAS Chamber Ensemble

PART II

RISING

CHAPTER 8

WHEN IT RAINS

I had once thought that the magic lay in the color of the fields or the sound of the wind, but my youthful notions had distorted the truth. The color returning to my dad's face and the enlivening sound of his voice bore the true foundation to my happiness. I loved Uihlein Soccer Park, not for its white posted stadium goals or the walls that I tried to label my own, but for the hours I spent playing soccer, all for the man who taught me everything.

—SEPTEMBER 27, 2017, A HIGH SCHOOL
CREATIVE ENGLISH PAPER

Fifteen first-grade girls in orange and navy-blue jerseys huddled under a tree near the sideline. The rain was falling in massive sheets, drenching our socks and shoes before the game had even started. Most parents had packed up their folding chairs and stood in a clump under umbrellas. Unlike everyone else, my dad was beaming.

"This is English weather!" he declared in a convincing British accent, dropping a few cones onto the field. Most girls were shivering miserably under their raincoats. Some were complaining about the mud accumulating underneath their cleats. The field was practically a swamp, boggy grass squishing with every step. One girl was crying.

"Alright, everyone on the line!" My dad was soaked, but he paced across the sideline, smiling and ready to make a point. An audible groan emerged from the team as a row of braids and pigtails formed on the white line.

"Okay, I want everyone to run as fast as you can to the other side," he shouted over the roaring rain. "When you get there, I need you to slide on your stomach with your hands out, like this!" He gestured how to execute the slide, with his hands outstretched and his face toward the sky.

"But we're gonna get all muddy," one girl said, recoiling in disgust.

My dad laughed and pointed a "spot on" finger at her. "Exactly," he said. "That's the fun of it."

As he blew the whistle, my teammates and I took off running, trudging across the field toward the sideline. The mud coated my entire body, spraying my socks, shoes, jersey, and face. I looked up as mortified parents watched their daughters purposely slide into the puddles of dirt.

We ran back toward my dad, who stood smiling with his arms crossed over his chest. Some girls had taken his instructions more seriously than others, covered in mud from head to toe, while others were hardly dirty. Giving all of us a once-over, he pointed to the other side of the field.

"Alright, again!"

Most of my teammates shifted uncomfortably in their shoes, now completely saturated with water. I wiped my muddy fingers on my raincoat and turned around, ready to run. We pumped through the grass as the mud squished beneath our cleats, sprinting toward the parents and eventually catapulting our tiny bodies into the earth. Some girls started to laugh, and when we jogged back to our starting spot, he made us do it again.

By game time, all fifteen of us were plastered with mud. The rain continued to drown the field, but we were giggling and embracing the downpour, even playfully smearing dirt onto our faces.

Looking at his team of waterlogged and muddy first-graders, my dad smirked. "Now you're ready to play."

THE REWARD OF RELENTLESSNESS

As my junior year of high school soccer commenced, unexpected tragedy transformed the meaning of our season.

Before practice began one afternoon, our coaches called for a huddle and hung their heads with devastating news. Meghan Flannery, an alumna and former soccer player, had died suddenly in a car accident. Aside from our coaches, none of us knew her, but the words of her premature death weighed in the pit of my stomach. Someone so young, taken so soon.

Before games, we started writing her initials with black Sharpie on the backs of our hands: MH #16. There was something powerful about acknowledging the intention behind every victory and the lessons that came with losing. Whatever the outcome, we strove to honor Meghan, because that was what it meant to play. We all carried the responsibility to play for the people who came before us.

I met Meghan's mom for coffee one afternoon because I desperately wanted to know about the person her daughter was. Although losing a twenty-six-year-old daughter seemed so far removed from my experience, my curiosity was rooted in understanding how loss changes us. Because our season had been so centered around Meghan's legacy, I felt compelled to know more. While we sat together in the corner of a crowded Starbucks, Mrs. Flannery handed me a laminated prayer card with a picture of Meghan. She was stunning: long brown curls, a sparkly smile, and gorgeous green eyes framed perfectly in a petite face. She also looked just like her mother.

Underneath the picture was a quote from Maya Angelou. "This was one of her favorites," Mrs. Flannery said.

I would like to be known as an intelligent woman, a coura-geous woman, a loving woman, a woman who teaches by being.[11]

As we talked, she told me about Meghan's ambitious personality and her constant desire to grow. In high school, Meghan had been a phenomenal athlete, involved in cross country, basketball, and soccer. On the soccer field, she was unstoppable. Meghan could play any position, and her coaches often placed her wherever the team needed help—defense, midfield, or forward, she could do it all. She was a four-year starter, and in 2008, she scored the game-winning goal for the state championship.

Mrs. Flannery told me about her daughter's unique ability to lead quietly by example. Meghan was a sweet, shy girl with a fearless love for adventure. Her coaches and teammates were constantly impressed by this silent strength.

When she graduated high school, Meghan knew she wanted to continue her soccer career and found herself

---

11 "16 Unforgettable Things Maya Angelou Wrote and Said," Glamour, Megan Angelo, accessed February 19, 2020.

playing for a Division 1 team at the University of Wisconsin–Madison. Her athletic ambitions were not limited to one sport. Upon graduating, Meghan decided to run a marathon. Like all her accomplishments, she finished with a triumphant smile, qualifying for the Boston Marathon.

Meghan also possessed a deep love for language. As a child, she was a voracious reader, absorbed by the *Harry Potter* series and eventually delving into the works of Maya Angelou. This passion for words led her to pursue an English language and linguistics major. However, after receiving an undergraduate degree, her plans changed. Meghan spontaneously applied for Teach for America, a nonprofit organization for people looking to make a difference in the education system. After a five-month training program, she obtained her master's degree in secondary education and teaching and then moved to St. Louis, Missouri, to serve as an elementary math teacher for kids in the inner city. I could see the pride brimming from Mrs. Flannery's eyes as she traced her daughter's countless successes. "Wow," I repeated several times, lacking adequate words for my admiration. I didn't have to know Meghan to know that she was beyond talented.

Mrs. Flannery told me that this redirection in Meghan's life was not part of her original plan, but she felt a calling toward this opportunity. Meghan was naturally good at math and knew there were kids who needed support. For the following two years, she worked in an under-resourced public school to help change the trajectory of children's lives.

During her time with the organization, Meghan came to see the systematic problems underway and the role they played in her students' experiences. Two years had completely changed her perspective, and she wanted to do more. Collaborating with the city's alderman, Meghan co-founded North Campus, an organization to serve as a liaison between students and educational success. She became the director of the program's Learning Center, where she hired and trained staff for tutoring services. I shook my head, mouth agape in awe and fascination. Meghan seemed like the definition of potential. She had tapped into this limitless potential, but she still had so much ahead in her future.

I asked Mrs. Flannery about her daughter's passing, carefully combing through my words, sensitive to the difficulty of sudden death. She cupped her chai latte, took a deep breath, and told me. On March 29, 2017, a devastating car accident took her life. A woman with talent and ambition and zeal for the world . . . somehow gone much too soon.

Together, Mrs. Flannery and I talked about the galaxy of emotions wrapped up in grief: the sorrow, the brokenness, the pining for hope, the emptiness, the loss of her child and her child's future. How do you recover from such a trauma?

In addition to this spectrum of emotions, Mrs. Flannery told me about the physical pain she experienced. I thought of all the times I had found myself crouched over on the bathroom floor, tears bleeding from my eyes and my stomach in an agonizing knot. The times when I found myself paralyzed, hyperventilating, clawing at the air, kicking the walls around me. With the tightening in my chest, I had finally understood why it was called heart-wrenching pain. "It was just unimaginable," Mrs. Flannery said. "I don't know if anything can be more devastating."

She continued by telling me about her gravitation toward faith for comfort. I stared at the new St. Benedictine bracelet on my wrist that she had given me a few minutes earlier. We had just met, but through our losses, we were quickly connecting with each other. The bracelet had come with an inspirational card that read, "In time of need, run your fingers along the simple chain; grasp the medal and breathe. By simply focusing our attention on taking a breath and linking that breath back to God, we can dispel chaos and go back to our spiritual roots."

Mrs. Flannery had a compelling gift for talking about her faith; maybe it was her palpable strength, or maybe it was just the way she talked about Meghan with such love and pride. I truly admired her ability to find consolation in religion. She talked about reading and praying, and simply observing the tiny gifts that life seemed to offer each day.

"I love when people talk about her," Mrs. Flannery continued, thinking about the stories she heard from Meghan's friends over the years. I agreed; there was something special about sharing memories of loved ones. So often I had seen people tiptoe around my dad's death, afraid to ask about the person he was. I had even caught myself holding back stories, so I wouldn't have to acknowledge his passing. I thought that this elephant in the room—a consequence of loss—was the norm, but no one told me that death didn't have to be clouded in shame. After all, loss was far out of our control, so why did we politely avoid the topic just to preserve other people's comfort? No one told me you can still talk about your loved ones as frequently and vibrantly as if they were here. No one told me sharing stories with others is integral to keeping their memory alive.

"I love when people say her name," Mrs. Flannery said, and I made a mental note. I would be sure to say her name whenever I got the chance.

We sifted through more details about her experience, covering the difficulties of grief, particularly about losing a child. She told me more about Meghan's fiery passion for life and her ability to seize every moment. With countless accomplishments in every area of her life, she seemed like the perfect example of what it means to heed your calling and chase your future. "I really wish I could have met her," I said, studying Mrs. Flannery's smile, which bore a striking resemblance to the picture of Meghan. With a small piece of her daughter's physical characteristics before me, I was getting a visual grasp of Meghan, one that reminded me how we all carry pieces of the people we have lost.

When I left that day, the warmth of Mrs. Flannery's hug prompted thoughts about my own purpose, a calling to keep chasing my dreams while I could. Mrs. Flannery's wisdom—her faith and willingness to talk about her daughter—was a testament to Meghan's legacy. I would never know Mrs. Flannery's pain or her exact experience, and I didn't understand a lot of things, like why grief aches so much and why a twenty-six-year-old would die with such a brilliant future ahead of her. But there were some things I did understand, or at least I could relate to: the shock, the emptiness, the devastation, the physical pain, the longing. Our losses were vastly different, and still, an unspoken understanding hummed between us. I could have talked for hours and hours with Mrs. Flannery, but I knew that with grief like this, we didn't need words at all.

With Meghan at the forefront of our minds, we battled through the season. Our coaches developed a running theme that it was our responsibility to play for those who came before us. Every game, we had fastened Velcro straps around our shin guards, black straps with a green cancer ribbon—our "Hegs" bands—to honor another player, Sarah Hegarty. This quiet memorial had become a tradition and was a visual reminder that we were always playing for something greater. Now, we wrote Meghan's initials on our hands and took the field to honor her legacy too.

Before one of our final games, my Coach Rob, who was himself a writer at heart, concluded an email with a few words that resonated with me:

When you take the field tonight, the rest of the season, and for the rest of your life, remind yourself how lucky you are to be on a soccer field competing. Remind yourself that recovering after a turnover, a missed shot, getting up off the ground, surviving a tough tackle, and overcoming mistakes is an honor and a gift. Remind yourself, being relentless is an every day, every hour, and every minute endeavor. The reward of relentlessness is the reward of truly being alive.

When I saw this, I put it everywhere. I printed it out, stuck it on our fridge, put it as my phone lock screen. I never wanted to forget those beautiful words.

Throughout the season, Meghan Flannery's legacy remained a burning motive not just to win, but to give every game everything we had. I was determined to commemorate her with every minute I spent on the field.

LOSSES WITHIN LOSSES

When I started my senior year of high school soccer, almost everything felt like a ticking time bomb for my grief. Stepping on the field was a trigger, and hearing parents cheering on the sidelines made me nauseous. My dad had been my biggest supporter and greatest inspiration, my coach and role model in every way. As a result, soccer and his absence were completely inseparable.

My teammates and coaches became the undying support I needed to get through the season. For every game, we would all write my dad's initials, "PS," in black Sharpie on the back of our hands. Before I took the field, I would trace the letters on my hand, whisper a soft prayer, and beg him to help me play well.

Still, I was so dissatisfied with the way I was playing. My touch was angry, scrappy; I would grit my teeth, fouling other girls and overcompensating my runs in frustration. My every move was one hundred miles an hour as I threw my body into other players and into the ground. When I stepped onto the field, my emotions suddenly broke lose, running rampant through my blood every minute of the game. I thought I had control over my grief, but soccer made the pain irrepressible.

I was exhausted, too, with the physical aftermath of grief taking its toll on my body. Sprinting up and down center-midfield, I would find myself completely out of breath, on the verge of hyperventilation. In part, I had hardly slept or eaten normally, but I knew it was mostly because when I stepped onto the open field, his absence was suffocating.

Sometimes, I would come off the field, break down into my palms, and chug some water before trying to recollect myself. My Coach Kevin would call my name and pat the number fourteen on my back—my dad's number—while we waited for the sub change. "Go be you, Sanchez," he said, and I would run back under the lights, praying that I could play like myself again.

When we reached the regional finals of our season, the pressure of winning hung over our heads like an ominous dark cloud. It was an unspoken standard that this was the year we would win; this was the season we all deserved a victory in pursuit of something greater. So when the whistle blew to start the first half, I ran as if my life depended on it. In many ways, it did.

Ninety minutes later, we were tied with the opposing team, heading into a dreaded overtime. Everyone felt the weight of the pressure, but I was fully distraught. I could not bear to lose anything else. When we found ourselves still trapped in a tie, facing a competition of penalty kicks, I was determined to salvage this game with whatever I had left in me.

All of us huddled together at the halfway line, with our arms wrapped around each other, holding our breath. Five of my teammates stepped to the white dot and fired a shot at the goal. I covered my eyes, begging for a win. Please God, please God, please, I whispered. I knew it was just a game, but to me it was everything.

After five shots, we were still tied. Coach Kevin paced in front of us. A sixth teammate shot, and the ball barely snuck its way into the lower right corner. We breathed, temporarily. The seventh shot found its way to the back of the net. Still tied. My coach stood in front of me and put a supportive hand on my shoulder. "Sanchez, I hear you've never missed in practice."

I wanted to puke. Taking a penalty kick in such a high-pressure game, with so many spectators and so many possible outcomes, was frankly my worst nightmare. I knew he was right, and I needed to do this, for myself and for my dad. After a nervous laugh, I inhaled for seven long seconds. Dad, I trust you, I thought, closing my eyes for a moment. Exhaling, I jogged to the eighteen-yard box. I could feel a hundred eyes full of pity trace my every outline. I've got this. C'mon Dad, let me make this. The defining memory of our season rested on this very moment.

The referee blew his whistle, and I could hear my dad's voice in the back of my head: Body over the ball, Nat. Hit it like you mean it. I delayed my run for a few seconds and locked eyes with the goalie. I glanced in the opposite direction that I intended to shoot, my rehearsed attempt to mislead her dive. You got this, my internal dialogue repeated.

I ran at the ball, shot it toward the lower right corner, and missed.

The goalie had caught it in a triumphant dive and rose her fist in the air while the other team rallied around one another. It was their turn, and if they made it, our season was over. I watched with tears in my eyes as a girl confidently stepped to the little white dot, cocked her head back, and scored.

After the whistle blew, I let myself fall apart. Was it possible to lose so much at once? Sinking to my knees, the sounds of cheering players from the opposing team and my sobbing teammates dissolved into a mere ringing in my ears. It wasn't fair; it just wasn't fair. I fell to the ground, drawing further and further into myself. Those familiar eyes of pity were everywhere, and I did not want to see them.

As I maneuvered past the groups of students and parents lingering outside the field, I wondered what my dad might have thought and what he would have said. Soccer was part of his whole life. It was one of his greatest passions, one he had instilled in my brothers and me from the time we were born. But at its core, I think that my dad thought soccer was a metaphor of sorts for life. He always believed that adversity builds character. That wins and losses are a part of life, and that fear of failure is more detrimental than failure itself. He knew challenges abound in life, but there was never a reason to give up and always a reason to leave everything out on the field.

Although we may not have won on the scoreboard, we most certainly did not lose, I wrote in my journal that night. *With every tackle, every goal, every mistake, and every moment on the field in pursuit of something greater, we won.*

That day still haunts me, mostly because the entire outcome of a season was subject to a few missed goals. But now I can see so clearly that losing did not affect the integrity of our season, or the integrity of anything in life, for that matter. I now realize that winning would not have changed our ability to play for my dad and for Meghan Flannery. The game was not about the results, but the reasons we played. It was about the ability to give it your all, regardless of personal struggle and heartbreak. It was about riding the victories and learning from the losses. It was about spending every waking second honoring the people who came before us.

A MESSAGE IN MUSIC
"There You'll Be" by "Faith Hill

CHAPTER 9

THE THINGS WE CAN CONTROL

———

Time softens many things, but not grief. The pain of loss is something that neither words nor time can possibly heal, only allow us to make room in our hearts for the good things in life.
—JANUARY 9, 2019, A LETTER TO MY FATHER

Wandering around an art exhibit in a hospital was not how I envisioned my Tuesday afternoon, but as I studied each piece, I found myself captivated by the shapes, colors, and beautiful interpretations of the human experience. Framed paintings and drawings were arranged on the largest wall: a vibrant flower bursting with oranges and yellows, a woman clothed in feathers, a snapshot of an empty chair in a living room—all created by cancer patients.

The room was massive, but the art filled every wall and covered every table. An enormous window on the far side of the room welcomed the whitish glow of an afternoon

sun, casting a natural spotlight onto the artwork. I lei-
surely inched along the wall, pausing often to study the
illustrations and read the names of the artists. One piece
in particular caught my attention: a white lab coat dis-
played on a stand with intricate words and drawings on
the back. *How I Got Here!* it said in bubbly blue letters,
surrounded by the detailed depictions of organs entwined
with arrows and tubes and the lengthy name of a diagnosis. The patient had drawn the hospital's logo, along with
a number: 371, perhaps a room number or the amount of
days spent battling their illness. *All lab coats should carry
powerful imagery like this,* I thought.

The most vibrant sketch, of a woman with compelling eyes
and a genuine smile, rested on an easel in the corner. It was
Kim Lese. I had seen her face many times before, beaming
from its permanent place on our kitchen fridge, where my
parents had decided to display her funeral program, but this
drawing was different. On this paper, she was so . . . alive.

As I followed the line of people into a smaller side room, I
nodded my head in acknowledgment to a middle-aged man
standing proudly over his creation: an intricately painted,
rainbow-colored wooden bench. "I have autism," he said with
his head held high. "I made this all by myself."

The smaller room contained pieces from grade-school
students Kim had taught as an art teacher and kids in her
children's grades. Among them was a striking stained glass
with colors that felt like Heaven. Backdropped by a soothing
blend of yellows, blues, pinks, and purples, the trunk of a
glowing tree stood as the foreground, and the corner of a
speckled sun bled into the other hues.

There were hundreds of other art pieces. Many of them were embellished with theme words—peace, love, joy, God. Some were detailed portrayals of Heaven and others were simple splatters of color, but I could see the grief and hope spilling onto each canvas. All the indescribable experiences that accompanied pain were lined up next to one another so neatly; the beauty and growth that could come from over-powering loss and sickness seemed tangible in those shapes and colors. I continued to roam around the gallery, hands stuffed in my jacket pockets, craning my neck to truly absorb each piece. Art was a beautiful, powerful translation from feeling to image.

When someone signaled for a speech, I followed everyone toward the front of the room and made myself comfortable on the carpet. I sipped a Sprite as sixteen-year-old Aidan Lese stepped up to the raised platform and unfolded a crumpled piece of paper.

The moment transported me to a day two years earlier. My dad was still here, and Kim had recently died. While sitting in a pew at the back of the church, I had watched Chris Lese and his three kids walk down the aisle together. Our pastor said a prayer, and then one of the boys from Aidan's grade handed them all an art piece: a giant heart with colorful notes and drawings. I had felt myself unintentionally star-ing, feeling broken for this family and these kids who had just lost their mom. My throat had risen in my chest while I held back tears. Kids so young didn't deserve that. No one deserved that. The following night, my dad hung his head before dinner, gesturing for us to hold hands. "Let's say a prayer for the Lese family," he said, and as we clasped hands around our dining room table, I couldn't fathom the thought of losing someone.

I could still picture Aidan from that day with floppy brown hair, walking beside his younger brother and sister to receive thoughtful messages from his classmates. He and his siblings had seemed so small then, and now Aidan stood a few feet in front of me, nearly two years older. It was a glaring reminder of the way time relentlessly carries on. My brothers, too, had changed in such a short amount of time. They had sprouted several inches, gaining deeper voices, the beginning signs of stubble appearing on their chins. Dominic's sudden muscular figure, Gabe's braces-less face, Luke's mature humor, the way I now had to look up at them instead of down—they were visual representations of all my dad was missing. They were growing up before my very eyes, and all I could think was that my dad was supposed to be here.

As I shifted my weight on the carpet, I thought about how Kim was also supposed to be here. I looked to my left and saw Audrey and Nathaniel, her two other kids, listening intently as their older brother spoke.

Earlier in the day, my mom had complimented Audrey on her denim dress and then told her it looked just like mine. "It does," I had agreed, smoothing the wrinkles in my dress, staring at this little girl almost half my age. We were so far removed from each other in age and experience, and yet loss made us more alike than I had ever realized. I felt a longing pang in my chest. Of all the things to have in common, why this?

Life was unfair for the obvious reasons, but also for specific reasons like a sixteen-year-old boy standing on a raised platform, commemorating his mom through shaking hands.

It was unfair for reasons like a little girl in a denim dress, spending her Tuesday afternoon at an art gallery in memory of her mom. And for reasons like the way I somehow understood their heartache without any words at all.

"Thank you all for coming here today to honor my mom," Aidan said, glancing from his paper to the crowd. As he moved through his speech, he spoke about his mom and her passion for art, her kindness, and her inspirational love for life. For eight years, she had battled cervical cancer, and with her son standing before us, I could see she was wildly courageous. Publicly acknowledging a loss was vulnerability in its finest form, and Aidan was emulating that courage as he carefully selected his words. I could remember the nervousness I felt the day I eulogized my dad. I had seen the crowd's eyes of pity, tinged with love and compassion and fascination; I wondered if Aidan noticed those same eyes too.

I moved my focus back to the sketch of his mom's face on the easel. There were soft wispy pencil strokes for her hair, convincing cross-hatching for a scarf around her neck, the perfect highlight on her lower lip. In the upper corner of the frame, I could see a reflection in the glass of the windows behind me. The sun was shining brilliantly into the room, casting its rays onto Aidan and the artwork like it was Kim herself. Again, I remembered that same feeling of my dad's presence while speaking to the church before me. Although I had been anxious to read my tribute before hundreds of people, I could sense something beyond words guiding me through the page.

When we left the hospital that day, I felt compelled to know more about Kim. I knew that while Aidan and his siblings were grieving the loss of their mother, there was an element of unspoken understanding between us. I could feel a strange gravitation toward the Lese family, as we both faced the galaxy of grief, caught in the same orbit around perpetuating loss. Somehow, we were moving at similar rhythms, in endless circles until our paths intertwined.

I exhaled, stepping out of the same hospital doors where I heard the news that changed my life, only a year before.

A CALL TO REMEMBER

Aidan and I went to a Starbucks one afternoon, because apparently meeting people with devastating losses for coffee was becoming the norm for me. Of all the things that might be shared over a cup of coffee, I thought, death was becoming my topic of choice.

We ordered our drinks; Aidan asked for a water, instantly reminding me that he was only sixteen years old. "I'm not much of a coffee person," he politely declined, and I was internally hitting myself for bringing a teenage boy to "get coffee." We sat at a high table while he sipped his ice water and I obligatorily sipped a strawberry lemonade—less adult than coffee, I reasoned, trying to will a sense of comfort into Aidan.

I wanted our exchange to feel like a mere conversation so I prefaced it with, "Feel free to ask me anything too." I needed him to know I was also still seeking hope and understanding. I had prepared myself with questions beforehand, hoping that, with the right words, I could get him to open up to me, but I quickly learned I didn't have to draw the responses out of him. Impressed by his willingness to share, I could sense

Aidan relaxing into the conversation, telling me openly about his experience without any prodding at all.

As we talked, I observed a notable sense of wisdom and maturity about him. He was honest and articulate about his pain, and I could see he was intuitive beyond his years. We talked about his mom, and the eight years she was sick; I found myself curious about the differences in our experiences. My dad's life had been stolen in a single moment, one final breath, but Kim had been dying with every breath, suffering through almost a decade of sickness. I asked Aidan if this slow deterioration had affected him as a child, but he just said, "Growing up, I hardly noticed."

His mom had been sick almost his entire childhood. I thought about how strong Kim must have been, for her son to reflect on the last eight years of his life so pragmatically. It was all too obvious that for those difficult eight years, she just wanted her children to have a normal upbringing with memories they could always cherish. Making pancakes for the kids, going through chemo, picking them up from school— these actions were the epitome of strength.

Talking to Aidan about losing his mom stirred several emotions in me. Although I was grateful for our shared under-standing, I also hated the world for conspiring to connect us in such a way. Kim was supposed to be here, but instead, I was sitting in a coffee shop with her sixteen-year-old son, sipping strawberry lemonade and talking about death.

Aidan told me how many of his friends didn't even know about his mom. I could relate, on a much different level, as my freshman year of college had felt like months of carrying a gigantic secret on my shoulders. I was constantly caught between the responsibility of keeping my dad's memory alive and fear of making my new friends uncomfortable. Grief was heavy enough as it was, but navigating the "reveal" element was another dimension that complicated loss. Aidan's struggle to tell his friends twisted my heart into a knot. When people lost someone, they deserved to cry about it from the rooftops.

We discussed coping mechanisms. In the early stages of grief, Aidan had preoccupied himself with schoolwork and exercise. "I get really fixated on things," he told me. "At one point, I was running ten miles a day." I envisioned my brother Gabe, walled up in his room, studying for hours on end, hunched over his laptop, engrossed in his social studies homework. I could see him setting up a punching bag in our basement, ready to sweat away the anxieties weighing on his heart. Looking at Aidan and the paper straw wrapper he had torn up into little pieces, I realized that navigating grief might be more about manifesting the few things we could control.

He continued telling me about his mom, describing her as "very outgoing." Throughout her career as a grade-school art teacher, she often coordinated exhibits and shows for her students at the Milwaukee Art Museum. Outside of her job, Kim and a friend performed puppet shows for children at various schools and libraries. I envisioned a room of kids laughing as she knelt behind a stage, assuming different characters and voices. Her lighthearted nature sounded so much like my dad. All his magic tricks were rooted in similar intentions to Kim's puppet and art shows. Like Kim's investment in her students, my dad loved coaching because he wanted to help kids uncover their talents and passions.

When Kim died, shock consumed the Lese family. Although she had been sick for many years, they did not know how near her passing truly was. In a matter of days, Kim's health worsened, and on May 23, 2017, she took her last breath. Anger with a hint of guilt bubbled inside me. We had both lost parents far too young, but there were still several milestones that my dad witnessed, that Kim would never see: graduating grade school, moving to high school, homecomings and proms, and college applications. There was no shortage of things my dad would miss—the beginning of college, the end of college, my wedding, my kids—but I still had him longer than Aidan had Kim.

Aidan brought my mind back to a positive place: "My dad and I were talking in the car one day, thinking of ways we could memorialize my mom, and I said an art show," he told me. At sixteen years old, Aidan knew what kind of tribute would best capture and commemorate his mom. After suggesting the idea, he volunteered to speak at the art show. It was a brave decision, but I suppose grief beckons some of us to do things we never thought we could. Aidan and his dad decided to hold the art show at the hospital Kim had gone to for treatment all the years before. If they were going to memorialize Kim, the venue, the art, and the speeches all had to live up to her legacy in every way.

Featuring exhibits from students and current patients, Aidan took the lead and planned the art show. For the entirety of the conversation, I forgot Aidan was four whole years younger than me. His honesty and poise were without question, a reflection of Kim and his desire to emulate her best qualities. I could see some of myself in him. Being the oldest child held a certain pressure and responsibility, but together we were tirelessly striving to honor our parents' lives.

As we wrapped up our conversation and headed to the car, I felt like I was reaching Aidan. Or maybe he was reaching me. My intention had been to learn about him, and I did, but Aidan unknowingly taught me that I was in control over my life and the way I chose to grieve.

When I pulled up next to his house to drop him off, I knew that connecting with people would carry me through the unpredictable road ahead. Even though the heartbreak and emptiness were wearing at my soul, the relationships I had formed with other people because of grief were invigorating. There were endless things out of my control. I couldn't limit the tears, the troubling thoughts, or the triggers of my dad's absence, but sharing experiences over a cup of coffee (or strawberry lemonade) was wholly in my power.

A MESSAGE IN MUSIC
"There Will Be A Light" by Ben Harper, The Blind Boys of Alabama

CHAPTER 10

MOMENTS WITH MEANING

Every day it's harder still. Not sure how to carry on with this emptiness in my heart.

—MARCH 16, 2018

My brother Dominic climbed under the covers next to me. I leaned back into the pillow, balancing my laptop on my knees and sifting through Spotify. It had only been nine hours.

"I can't believe he's really gone," he said, nestling closer to me.

"Me neither."

"It just feels like a really bad dream, like I'm gonna wake up and it'll be a nightmare."

"I know."

He was right. That's exactly what it felt like.

The previous nine hours of my life had been inconceivable. I didn't want to fall asleep because I was afraid of what I might find in the morning—that everything was real.

We spent the remainder of the night collecting songs and crafting an extensive playlist that embodied my dad in every way. It had all his favorites: Rush, Phil Collins, The Samples, Tom Petty, Bob Marley, John Denver, The Beatles, Van Morrison—there were hundreds. Every song seemed to encapsulate a memory.

I pictured my dad somehow playing a perfect rendition of "Eruption" by Van Halen on an acoustic guitar.

Memories of him singing me a lullaby of "Surfer Girl" by The Beach Boys came floating into my mind.

"Wonderful Tonight" by Eric Clapton reminded us of my dad performing the song for my mom at their wedding.

I could still hear him toggling with the keyboard in our basement, trying to learn Frankie Valli and the Four Seasons' "December, 1963 (Oh, What a Night)" by ear.

I even remembered him showing me OK Go's music video for "This Too Shall Pass" when I was eight or nine years old. He had been fascinated by the single three-minute shot of the Rube Goldberg Machine.

We added song after song after song, eventually developing a playlist almost seventeen hours long. To anyone else, it might have seemed excessive, but my dad was made of music. Among all the things he left behind, his favorite songs felt like a portal to wherever he was. Only hours after his soul had flown far from his body and into the unknown, these songs took on an entirely new meaning. It was a precious playlist, one that conjured sacred memories of my dad in his happiest moments.

From that night on, music became everything: a connection with my dad, catharsis, an escape. I learned quickly that there were very few things so transformative. For every emotion I encountered, there was a song, and for all the words I couldn't find, there were lyrics that spoke deeply to me. However, there were still elements of my experience, all the things that make it uniquely me, that I needed to shape into music.

THE LAST CHRISTMAS

I've become fascinated with the way loss transforms our most ordinary moments into crystal-clear imprints of memory. It turns the mundane into treasures, gives pieces of our past immense value solely because they were the last. A casual voicemail, a piece of handwriting, a hug—they all melt into a collection of holy grail memories after loss. What's even more incredible is that some moments were meant to be for a reason. Tragedy happens, death is unavoidable, but in the pockets of these deep losses are fragments of hope.

Our last Christmas as a family was sewn together by some of those pieces, and as I reflect on December 25, 2017, I feel blessed to know everything on that day occurred because goodness is also inevitable. Life is a constant yin and yang of darkness and light; wherever there is pain, there is also an underlying gift to remind us that good things, too, still exist.

As the six of us unknowingly cozied around the tree together for the last time, my dad perched his boom box on our china cabinet and turned up the oldies Christmas station. While Nat King Cole's voice warmed the room, we sat together for the entirety of "The Christmas Song."

"Oh, wait, one more thing!" My dad stood up from his spot on the love seat next to my mom and started rummaging through the coat closet. He hauled out a clunky, haphazardly wrapped four-foot object, with the top of a guitar case peeking through the wrapping. He lugged it across the living room and gently placed it in front of me.

"Hmmm, I wonder what it is," I teased. The wrapping paper came off in one piece and I looked at him, confused. I had wanted a guitar for years.

"Open it up!" he prodded, bursting with excitement.

I lifted the top of the case to reveal a sleek, light-grained acoustic Taylor with an ebony fretboard and dark brown Koa pickguard. Out of the corner of my eye, I could see my dad leaning in toward my reaction, beaming with pride. Gift-giving was his passion. The guitar fit flawlessly in my hands, and its weight sat comfortably in my lap. I didn't know any chords, but I strummed to hear its perfect tune.

"That's a very special guitar," he said. "Your mom gave that to me."

Prior to that Christmas, I never knew the significance behind any of my dad's guitars. "Thank you!" I stood up, wrapped my arms around his neck, and squeezed him. "I love it!"

"I love you," he said, kissing my cheek and then whispering into my ear, "But you better take good care of that."

Overwhelmed with excitement, I picked up the guitar again and held it in my lap. I was always an awkward receiver of gifts, with my voice somehow crawling up an octave and finding a timid inflection. "Thank you," I said again, a smile spreading across my face. "Why are you giving this to me?" In some ways, the gift seemed particularly random. Learning how to play the guitar had been a lifelong wish, so why now? I could see in his eyes that he was wholly insistent upon giving it away.

The image of his responsive smile is forever ingrained in my brain. "Because," he said, "I wanted you to have it."

MY FATHER'S GUITAR

Sitting in my bedroom with the guitar face up in its case generated that memory a thousand times over. Why had he given it to me less than three months before he died? It was almost as if my dad knew I would need that guitar more than anything in the entire world.

There seemed to be a series of these occurrences, precious moments contingent upon nudges from God. I didn't believe decisions such as this one and the timing of his death were mutually exclusive. Seemingly "random" choices had an important place in the universe, and the more I thought about their significance, the harder it became to ignore them. Only two days before my brother Dominic left for his Freshman Retreat, I had encouraged my family to write letters to him. My dad's letter included the last words Dominic would ever hear from him. It was undoubtedly a nudge from God.

Likewise, only months before my dad's passing, my parents went on a retreat together, where they wrote letters to each other in a notebook, strengthening their faith and marriage. Another nudge.

In his final year, my dad ensured that every one of his kids had a musical instrument to boost their passions. He gave Dominic an acoustic guitar, Gabe a drum set, and Luke a bass. These were prompts from something far beyond mere coincidence.

Just as I felt something external guiding these decisions, a strange musical connection among my uncles and I began to form. I clearly remember one night after my dad's passing, when I received a text from Uncle Eric, with an attached voice memo of a song he had written. Uncle Brian and I were both stunned; we had written songs too. The three of us were functioning on similar rhythms, writing what we felt to survive.

I spent most of my free hours after school and on weekends receiving guitar lessons from Uncle Eric. He helped me practice scales and perfect certain chords, but I felt a persistent twinge of what could have been. Uncle Eric had an extensive setup in his basement, with artist posters, walls with paneled wood, and neon lights above his instruments. The room's musical ambience was comforting, but without my dad, there was an undeniable element of hollowness.

Nevertheless, I was determined to learn how to play guitar. Whether I had made this promise more to myself or to my dad was indeterminable. After his death, that line was blurred by my personal notion that everything was for him: the soccer game, the calculus test, the song—every waking moment of my life became a pursuit in his honor. It was the only way I could find the strength to move through the motions of life.

So for hours upon hours, I heeded Uncle Eric and Uncle Brian's instructions, in a clunky, frustrated tempo of two steps forward, one step back. The learning curve was one obstacle, but the emotional weight of the guitar made some of the lessons too difficult to retain. When I couldn't master a bar chord in a few tries, my impatience would often leave me in a state of what some might called unreasonable devastation. One mistake was only a moment away from emotional implosion.

As the weeks went by, I picked up on certain verses or choruses but never mustered the patience to master an entire song. In a perfect storm of my restlessness and stubborn perfectionism, I usually ended up picking random snippets of songs to learn before moving to the next one. Robotically, I would pluck the beginning riff of "Wish You Were Here" by Pink Floyd, until my fingers were sore. Then I'd venture into some of Justin Vernon's early songs or play around with whatever music my uncles suggested. Most days were futile attempts to produce anything at all. My efforts always fell short of expectation, and I began wallowing in guilt for never asking my dad to teach me how to play.

Spending time with my dad's guitar consoled me to some extent. But when writing found its way into the equation, I dumped every thought and feeling onto paper. Music was cathartic, writing was cathartic, and together the two were healing. I wanted control over the words I sang, even if control meant replaying the same two chords over and over and over. For me, the music needed to reflect what was in my heart, and the only way to do that was to write it.

My uncles did the same. We shared our thoughts, sent voice recordings of our personalized songs, and gathered on weeknights to practice. I couldn't help but notice myself scanning the world for lyrical inspiration. It rained, and I thought of him. Butterflies floated past my window, and I had to journal about it. I would sit in school and daydream about a list of rhyming words to string together. For months, I could not stop writing.

One day, Uncle Eric mentioned a friend based in Chicago who had a home studio and an entire set of professional recording equipment. His suggestion was simple yet intimidating: the three of us could write and produce an album.

I agreed, still naive, amateur, and somewhat instrumentally incompetent in comparison to my uncles. They were both phenomenal musicians, and I spent most recording sessions wishing for talent like theirs. However, I knew the effort was what mattered the most, at least to me. Giving this one up to you, dad, I would repeat, my mantra for most things that felt out of my control. Giving this one up to you.

JUST THE SAME

On the first anniversary of his death, it rained. First a drizzle, then a light, foggy spray. My entire extended family had parked their cars on the gravel road near his grave, waiting for our informal commemoration to begin. When our pastor, Father Charlie, arrived, everyone huddled under umbrellas for a few prayers.

March 9, 2019, initiated a biting cold, with snowbanks rising to our calves. My mom and I had shoveled a small circle around his grave so everyone could stand together. As we shivered, clutching umbrellas and pretending to be unaffected by the negative temperatures, Father Charlie led a prayer. The second he got the first word out, the fine rain grew into a torrential downpour. A draft of wind rustled the pages of his Lectionary, while my aunt dangled an umbrella over his head. The weather was absolutely unbearable, but for some reason, we all started to laugh.

"I can only imagine how many soccer games Paul coached in weather like this," Father Charlie projected through the rain. Everyone in my family shared a subdued, nostalgic laugh. The rain spilled onto the earth in pellets, and we recited the Our Father through chattering teeth and frozen lips.

We stood in the rain for only a few minutes longer before abbreviating the service and scattering a collection of red and white roses. I wondered how 365 days could have possibly come and gone. One year of waking and rising, waking and rising. Fifty-two weeks of changing seasons, evolving lives.

Everyone climbed into their cars and regathered at Uncle Brett and Aunt Sheri's house, where we celebrated with music and food (piña coladas and Greek fries from my dad's favorite restaurant). Uncle Eric and Uncle Brian set up a microphone and amplifier in the center of the living room, with hopes for the three of us to perform a song from the album. I sensed a subconscious resistance to play, mostly rooted in my fear of failing. It had to be perfect.

The two of them said a few words and played their songs for the entire room of family and friends. My cousins and some friends sat cross-legged with me on the floor. When my turn came, I awkwardly shuffled to the front of the room, slung the guitar over my shoulder, and leaned into the microphone.

"So a couple months ago," I began, "my mom told me to write a letter from my dad's perspective." Everyone leaned in toward me, and I avoided making eye contact through my shaky voice. "So I decided to do that, in the only way I know, which is a song." Instantly cringing, feeling cliché, I took a deep breath and strummed a flimsy G.

When your legs give out
And you feel alone
My open arms
Will guide you home

The guitar was out of tune, but I stared at the ground and sang over my imperfect execution.

When you can't move on
And you're losing sleep
When your strength is gone
You can fall on me

I could sense the same tension from everyone in the room in the same way I did at his funeral. Forty people holding their breath for me, silently hoping I could relieve them with my confidence. Although I didn't feel particularly nervous, the physical manifestations of anxiety began to rise within me. The truth was, I did not care as much how I performed for those people in the room, but for my dad, it had to be flawless.

When the years don't stop
And the sun goes down
When you're all grown up
And you leave this town

Playing an extra round of chords to control my breathing, I finally closed the song with the chorus.

You can feel me in the rain
In the wind against your face
I will speak in every heartbeat
And I'll love you just the same

The image was one I had avoided for a long time. The mere thought of being "grown up" seemed so foreign and far away, but then again, my childhood was nearly a decade ago. What would that ten-year-old have to say about my reality?

Everyone in the room clapped, but I was disappointed in myself. Nothing was ever going to satisfy my vision, but still, the song was nothing close to what I hoped. Shaky voice. Uneven chords. It always could be better.

My friend Margot wrapped her arms around me while I sank to the floor and hung my head in my hands. "I just wanted to make him proud," I muttered through pathetic tears. Grief somehow groomed everything for inadequacy, and my own efforts were no exception. Some would label it self-critical, but the frustration was just another symptom of loss. I, of course, knew he would be proud of me regardless of the outcome, but he deserved perfection: a perfect soccer game, a perfect calculus test, a perfect song; anything less felt like a failure.

Margot leaned in and squeezed me. "Nat, he is so proud of you. I know it."

A MESSAGE IN MUSIC
"Weight of the World" by The Samples

CHAPTER 11

A MOTHER'S
ETERNAL LOVE

———

There are endless things that serve as a constant reminder of your absence. It's impossible to imagine that the passing days will only add more time since you have been gone. But I guess that means I am one day closer to seeing you again.

—JULY 9, 2018, A LETTER TO MY FATHER

Most of the time, I never knew how to ask for help.

My struggle was primarily rooted in fear that my grief was a burden for others. The pain was so unbearable that I often took cover under the blankets in my bed, secretly hoping no one would find me. Besides not knowing how to ask for help, I didn't know what kind of help I needed. Avoidance felt like the only option, so I always hid somewhere, drawing deeper and deeper into myself and my grief.

My childhood best friend and roommate, Tess, always noticed when my subconscious had convinced me my pain was a burden. We had a sixth sense for each other, and somehow she always found me when I needed her most.

One night, when I had avoided the world and buried my face in the blankets, she crawled to the top of the bunk and lay down next to me. I had my headphones pressed into my ears, drowning out the silence with my dad's favorite songs. My cries were muffled by the fortress I had built of pillows and tissues. She touched my arm, and I recoiled, curling into a ball because I couldn't look her in the eye.

When she asked me why I wouldn't talk to her, I mumbled, "It's not fair you have to deal with this."

She shifted her weight on the mattress, leaned in, and hugged me. "Well, life isn't fair. It's unfair that we have to take math, it's unfair that I spilled my coffee this morning, and it's unfair that your dad died. And if this is the worst part of your life right now, that might mean it will be mine too, but that's okay. I want to do all that I can to carry that weight with you."

I emerged from the layers of blankets, smiling through puffy lips and ugly tears. I knew I was not prepared to carry the weight by myself . . . I was already crippled under the burden alone. I needed to trust her wisdom and remind myself that only so much strength could be drawn from within. Loss was about finding the people who love you and letting them take a tiny piece of the pain.

THE FIRST BREATH OF PRAYER

My dad peeked his head into each of our rooms and summoned the entire family to the living room. He paced back and forth, twisting the beads of a pearly white rosary between his fingers.

"Alright, guys, we are going to say a prayer for Stella." He dimmed the lights and invited us all to sit on the couch with him. My mom cradled Luke, then only three months old, sleeping peacefully on her chest. Although Dominic and Gabe were too young to understand the prayer or the intention behind it, and I was only in first grade, my dad was insistent on including the whole family. He was a man who believed in teaching everything through experience: executing the perfect soccer step-over, cooking the world's best chili recipe, and praying the Rosary as purposefully as possible. He knew the importance of teaching by example and believed it was never too early to develop strong values.

Prayers for the O'Neil family had been sweeping across our parish as hundreds of people bowed their heads for the recovery of their one-year-old. I had never prayed the Rosary before, and I did not understand how reciting a few ancient words over and over was conducive to a miracle, but nevertheless, I curled up next to my dad and studied his every move. With heavy eyelids and my head on his chest, I listened to the soothing pattern of Hail Mary's and Glory Be's until they softened into a calming invocation inseparable from my dreams.

ACHING FOR THE SAME REASONS

I reached out to Vanessa O'Neil to hear more about her perspective on grief. All I knew was that she had been through a much different kind of devastating loss, and the only concrete recollection I had of her story was my family sitting on the couch, praying the Rosary. The image of my dad's fingers slowly moving along its beads replayed in my head. I sat at the desk in my dorm, swiveling back and forth on the chair, racking my brain for details from that night. After a decade, the memory had softened a bit, but it was still there. Although our experiences were almost polar opposites, I expected Vanessa and me to connect in one way or another. I had learned that loss was another language, and I wanted to see just how far it would stretch.

I dialed Vanessa's number, doodling aimlessly on a scrap piece of paper. The ringer stopped, and we greeted each other, two somewhat strangers waiting to dive head-first into an honest conversation about life and loss. My parents had been friends with Vanessa and her husband, but at least in my humble memory, I could not remember the two of us speaking to one another. However, within those first few seconds, I sensed a certain familiarity about her voice. Maybe it was a faint memory resurfacing from the past, or maybe it was just that grief instantly acquaints us with people who understand.

Almost immediately, Vanessa expressed her condo-lences: "Your dad was such a great man," she said, and I was already swallowing the lump in my throat. "I couldn't believe when I heard it. I've been thinking about you guys ever since." I thought about how, even as an eight-year-old, the memory of Stella had left a profound imprint on my mind. In a quieter way, one that was gradually evolving as I grew up, I had been thinking of Stella all along.

I asked Vanessa about Stella, and from the other end of the line, I could sense she was eager to share. After a mere year, people had gradually stopped asking about my dad; I couldn't fathom the difficulties of grieving for eleven years, after the cards and casseroles and conversations had faded into silence. This struggle was a symptom of rebuilding ourselves after loss; as we grow and change and reshape our life, the pain becomes less obvious from the outside. The grief never dissipates. It's always there, guiding our daily thoughts and choices, but we learn to wear a mask. This façade is not a conscious attempt to hide the grief, but rather an outward representation of how we have familiarized ourselves with the pain. Hiding under a soft smile or a hearty laugh, the grief is always, always there.

Vanessa recounted January 2008, when Stella was nearing her first birthday. She and her husband, Brent, noticed Stella had been having trouble with basic motor skills and immediately took her to the emergency room, where she received a series of tests and scans. The results were shocking: stage four neuroblastoma cancer. I stopped spinning in my chair. The chest pain, the dangerous fevers, and complete loss of mobility—childhood cancer was appalling. How was it fair for a complex, incurable, and malignant disease like this to reach someone so young and vulnerable?

As the tumor grew in her spine, Stella began chemotherapy right away. In addition to the lethal cancer in her daughter's body, Vanessa told me that Stella had simultaneously contracted RSV (respiratory syncytial virus), a form of pneumonia in infants. She was then admitted into the PSICU (Pediatric Surgical Intensive Care Unit). I scribbled the big words onto my scraps of paper. So much painful terminology was wrapped up in her experience.

The doctors were working tirelessly to restore her health, but the implications from the medications were irreversible, with a devastating complication to each drug—one would make Stella infertile; another would cause hearing loss—Vanessa was overwhelmed by the massive amount of medical information to absorb. I could hear the sharp pains resurface as she said, "We never had a day where it went in the right direction."

Even eleven years later, Vanessa was still searching for the coping strategies to relay the complexity of her story. She was working to share the parts that left her feeling insecure; when people responded with a disturbed or uncomfortable facial expression, she instantly believed that she had overshared. But the gruesome details about her daughter slipping away from sickness made her story . . . her story.

I remembered the first time my mom uttered the words "cerebral hematoma." I had drilled the phrase into my brain. Staring at a blank Google search bar, I typed my dad's cause of death and waited for the results to materialize. With a morbid curiosity, I clicked through several websites, unsure if I actually wanted more details or if I was pining for proof that his death was real. I didn't want to know the reason, but without a reason, I was restless.

The words "cerebral hematoma" are just a part of my story. Although they are nowhere near as complicated as the medical jargon in Vanessa's experience, both of us were learning to integrate these terms into our narrative. Whether we spoke these words aloud or not, they were inevitably imprinted on our hearts.

The doctors put Stella on a ventilator, and Vanessa and her husband Brent kept vigil at their daughter's bedside, praying for her recovery. Brent remained hopeful by consistently posting on the family's Caring Bridge website and communicating with the hospital caregivers. While he was an optimist, Vanessa labeled herself the realist in their marriage, feeling completely helpless as she watched her daughter's health decline. "At that point, I was already falling apart," she told me.

For six grueling weeks, Vanessa and Brent spent day after day in the hospital. Stella spent her first birthday there, unconscious and clinging to life by ventilators. "We never got the chance to bring her home after that first treatment," Vanessa said. In a matter of weeks, the O'Neils' life had spiraled out of control into a dark void of desperation. I noticed a sinking sensation in my chest as Vanessa spoke. I was familiar with the sudden, unexpected type of loss, where a single second was the difference between life and death. But with cancer, the slow deterioration of a person was unexpected too. Vanessa never knew what the following day would bring for her daughter, and the constant unknown added another dimension to the grief.

I could hear Vanessa take a deep breath, and I somehow knew what she was going to tell me. In the leap year of 2008, they made the heartbreaking decision to turn off the machines. "They gave her every opportunity to start to get a little better," Vanessa recalled. "But at that point, she was pretty much just being kept alive by machines." The sinking sensation in my chest was now a knot, and suddenly I was scrawling tangled, tornado-like scribbles on my paper again. The why's and what if's of death never seemed to end.

Vanessa told me that the loss sparked a curiosity in her about eternal life. "When I lost Stella," she said, "it really shook my belief system about where you go." I nodded my head in agreement. You can believe in Heaven all your life, but when someone you love is supposed to be there, no amount of explanations can satiate your curiosity. "I went on this research journey," she began, and I smiled. For months, I had been consumed by YouTube videos about people who claimed to come back to life, documentaries about how science proved God was real, and books about what we would find in the afterlife. My quest for answers was never-ending, a pursuit to know for certain where my dad was and how he got there. "I really got into spirituality," Vanessa continued, "learning about souls, why souls come to Earth, and purpose."

The room abruptly grew a few degrees warmer. The sun had emerged from a few clouds, chasing away the shadows and casting a promising beam of light onto my papers. At the core of it all, Vanessa and I were searching for the same things and aching for the same reasons.

Grief took many forms, and every once in a while, these different manifestations of pain crossed one another, to remind us that we were going through wildly different, yet strangely similar experiences . . . together. I had lost my forty-six-year-old father, and she lost her one-year-old daughter, but we both were looking for hope, to soothe the empty hole inside our hearts. The aching could be felt in a million different forms, like Tess crawling to the top bunk and offering to feel the weight with me, or Vanessa, who understood the longing through experience. From one loss to another, we were all connected by the desire for answers and for hope.

Vanessa told me that losing Stella also transformed the way she perceived relationships with other people. "I had to accept that I had been through something traumatic and kind of unmentionable, and that meant it might be harder for me to socialize with other people," she said. "I started feeling like I needed to become more introverted and private." She paused for a while. "It's definitely hard because people in general don't want to talk about it or see it, because it's too scary to them." Craning my neck to pin the phone between my ear and shoulder, I twisted the ring on my index finger. When did grieving become so taboo? I could explain why people were afraid of loss, but when did people become afraid to talk about loss?

There were so many milestones Stella would never reach. Vanessa explained the longing "what could have been" pain that accompanies every year: little girls lined up in bright backpacks for the first day of school, tiny white dresses for First Communions, colorful flyers of the kids selling Girl Scout cookies. Endless triggers came with this kind of loss. For the rest of her life, Vanessa would be plagued by who Stella might have become. Suddenly I was drawing jagged, lightning-bolt-shaped lines along the margins of the paper. I knew who my dad had become; he reached adulthood and became a father. He was a soccer coach, a zealous musician, a talented magician. Although decades of his life were still left with a massive question mark, Vanessa would always wonder.

As we continued talking, she mentioned daily challenges I had never even considered, like how her oldest daughter

Maddie will always struggle with her identity: an only child or a girl who lost her sibling. Grief is strangely secretive. In a world that pressures people to "move on," time has become falsely synonymous with remedy. But time does not heal all things. The passing years just make us more inclined to hide the innermost parts of our stories.

Vanessa's strength inspired me for several reasons. She was excited to share her experience with me. She upheld an aura of positivity, despite the suffering in her life; she had a unique perspective on grief—because she had lost her mom too.

THE SECOND LOSS

In 2016, eight years after Stella's passing, her mother Linda was diagnosed with ovarian cancer. My eyebrows rose, lips pursed with the words of disbelief on my tongue. A hundred questions about fairness circulated through my head. Hasn't she been through enough? When Vanessa described the death of her mother, she reminded me that loss knows no boundaries. Heartache was lingering at every stage of life, the potential for tragedy always unknown. In the span of only eight years, while still grieving the loss of her daughter, Vanessa faced another difficult battle.

Her mom, Linda, was the epitome of a mother, always loving and always giving. She was a generous soul who often gave what Vanessa called "right from the heart kind of stuff"— little trinkets or treats for family and friends. Vanessa had a close relationship with her mom, one that especially grew after Stella's death. Linda became a championing source of support, always willing to talk about her granddaughter and giving Vanessa little ornaments with Stella's name for

Christmas. "She was the one who helped me grieve the most," Vanessa said, her words still raw.

For most of the year, Linda was relatively active and in decent health until six weeks of rapid decline. As her health plummeted, she started home hospice. Only two weeks later, at sixty-nine years old, she passed away. Although she was able to say goodbye, Vanessa felt deeply lost without her mother.

It had been a troublesome eight years, and Vanessa found herself in the middle of two extremes: losing a child and losing a parent. On the gigantic spectrum of loss, this was surely the center, the place she would come to know grief in more forms than one. The dichotomy between these two heart-wrenching losses left Vanessa to dissect the emotions she felt. "I've been able to compare and contrast the grief," she said, "and it has helped me to process the things I'm still working through with Stella."

Vanessa had a lifetime with her mother and only one year with her baby girl, but both losses broke her in different parts.

Although losing a parent at any age is a scarring wound, Vanessa found comfort in knowing that her mother was in her life for so long. With photos, clothes, and songs, countless moments reminded her of her mom's presence every day. "I have these memories. I have these artifacts. I have lots of things that I can think about with her," she said. I, too, didn't go a day without finding one of these reminders. Guitar picks, old T-shirts, playing cards, the photos covering my bedroom wall—time (even though it's never enough) gives us precious memories as gifts.

In stark contrast, losing a one-year-old child entailed an entire universe of emotions I couldn't comprehend. I thought about the one-year-olds I knew: little cousins, family friends, kids I babysat . . . they couldn't talk in full sentences and some still hadn't learned to walk.

"I feel like I missed so much of her short life," Vanessa said. The chaotic, early stages of motherhood had overwhelmed many of her memories, as the lack of sleep and feedings in the middle of the night comprised most of her time with Stella. During that first year, she rarely wanted to be in photos while recovering from pregnancy. "By the time I finally started feeling like I was getting back on my feet was when she started getting sick," she continued, voice tinged with longing. "I can't pull from a lot of memories, and it's really hard to work through when you don't have those memories."

Vanessa and I talked through our respective changes in perspective. "I'm trying to really honor my mom by being more like her," she said. "Someone who's loving, supportive, and nurturing." She and I shared a common goal of trying to embody the best qualities of the people we lost. Grief had challenged us to be kinder, more patient, more positive. Doing so was not easy, but for the two of us, it had become a personal mission.

This initial conversation became a baseline for a new friendship with Vanessa. She began texting me pictures of the little things she noticed throughout her day: a group of turkeys near Stella's grave, a plate of Christmas cookies made by her sister using Linda's old cookie cutters. Her thoughtful messages were uplifting, and I could feel her opening up to me a little more with each one. "My thoughts and feelings about loss have been actively evolving by reading your work," she said while she told me about her newfound sense of gratitude.

As Vanessa developed these new insights, she became increasingly aware of the people and blessings in her life, especially her sister, who frequently cares for Stella's grave.

While Vanessa and I shared sentiments, my thoughts and feelings were evolving too. As I contemplated my new perspectives, I still struggled to grasp the power of prayer. My dad had been committed to his faith and always encouraged us to talk to God, but doing so was hard and didn't make sense. We prayed an entire Rosary and Stella still died. So why keep praying?

* * *

I remembered a homily I once heard in church that was centered around this idea. Our priest, Father Charlie, had leaned over the pulpit, pausing between his words for effect. My mind usually drifted in and out of focus during Mass, but I was fixated on his message this time: "Do we pray to remind God of our needs, or do we pray to remind ourselves that we need God?"

I mentally rewound the moment and replayed those words again.

Do we pray to remind God of our needs, or do we pray to remind ourselves that we need God?

I then understood why my dad believed so deeply in prayer. Life wasn't fair and never would be. Grieving was forever, suffering was guaranteed, and God was there to carry our burdens with us. Reflecting on the night when my dad encouraged us to pray the Rosary, I sat in the pew with this epiphany, over a decade later.

Faith was hard to feel sometimes, but its purpose was to acknowledge that we could not carry our deepest pains alone. God sends us people—who love and understand us—to lighten our load when the weight is too much. Although it seemed that Vanessa's and my stories were only beginning to intertwine, they had interlaced years earlier. At eight years old, with my head on my dad's chest and my family sitting in a dimly lit living room, I was already inching closer to my connection with her. Through each passing year, we unknowingly moved toward the asymptote of understanding. We were both gradually learning how to ask for help, crawling through the motions until we stumbled upon each other again. This was not chance or conscious choice, but God, who knew we needed to share our stories.

A MESSAGE IN MUSIC
"Lullabye (Goodnight, My Angel)" by Billy Joel

CHAPTER 12

FINDING FAITH

———

I would like to make giving thanks an every minute endeavor because to search for the good in the darkest hours of life is the simplest way to find happiness. I am going to let the light in, let it begin today.

—DECEMBER 3, 2018, A LETTER TO MY FATHER

Toward the end of March, while most of my classmates were anxiously waiting to graduate, I found myself wholly distraught about choosing a college. Just when I had been daydreaming about the possibilities for my future, my world fell apart. My plans for the next chapter of my life were suddenly pulled from beneath my feet; everything felt unmanageable, unpromising, and unthinkable.

I was an indecisive person to begin with, but my dad's passing left me paralyzed. For months before, I had been fantasizing about what the next four years of my life would entail.

I had spent months dreaming.

At night, I would crawl under the covers and click through film school application videos, sometimes with tears in my eyes, secretly hoping one day I'd be behind a camera directing films of my own. I would doodle lists of cities I wanted to see in my planner, places I could envision myself: New York, Los Angeles, Minneapolis, Denver, St. Louis, the list stretched from coast to coast, most of them financially improbable, but the idea of moving far from home was enthralling.

The possibilities felt endless; I thought about being nurse, a psychologist, a filmmaker, a writer . . . for my naively ambitious mind, anything and everything was on the table. College soccer, too, lingered in the back of my head, a persistent question of whether I should continue playing after high school.

I voiced these internal battles out loud, badgering my parents for much-needed guidance and advice, but my dad usually just teased me. "But what about the rainbow house?" he always said. At seven years old, I had made stubborn plans to live with my parents forever in a rainbow duplex (picture the colorful Victorian house from the movie *Up*). "Are you sure you don't want to live with us forever?" He would elbow my shoulder, and I would return to college applications after rolling my eyes into an exaggerated face palm.

Maybe it was because I was an incurable romantic, or maybe graduating felt like the next step to unlocking my purpose; either way, I had big plans and even bigger dreams.

And then, suddenly, everything changed.

The big plans and the big dreams were off the table. They had been erased from my mind, shoved into a box, and tucked neatly into a corner of my heart I might never see again.

My desire to reinvent myself in the next chapter was gone. What reasons did I have to care? What reasons did I have to embrace change in any form? I had choices to make, but I didn't want them. What could decisions do to salvage what was left of my broken dreams?

The end of high school was approaching all too quickly, and every day brought a new reminder that I wasn't ready. My friends were itching to graduate, but every approaching milestone haunted me. Again, all I could think was that he was supposed to be here. For the ceremony, for the diploma, for the celebration dinner, for dropping me off in a dorm and saying, "See you at Thanksgiving." For the phone calls, the "I miss you" texts, the "I love you's" and the "I told you so's." For my first year of college, and the second, third, and fourth, for my wedding and my kids . . . he was supposed to be here.

But he wasn't, and as I stood in the shower, apathetically staring at my half-painted toenails and the water funneling into the drain, I thought: *Well, what now?*

I asked myself the same question while sitting in Kathleen Cullen's office during my lunch period the next day. She had been one of the first people to reach out to me. Although we had rarely spoken, I sensed an underlying empathy in her message that immediately set her words apart from anyone else. She was the Director of Campus Ministry, and I had spent the majority of my free periods in the cozy common area outside her room, napping on the couches or eating lunch, completely unaware she was living every day with loss.

* * *

After my dad died, Kathleen instantly undertook several projects. Considering she had a four-month-old son, I couldn't believe the measures she took to support me. She organized a meal delivery list for our family, then a prayer service at school. I had sat with my friends in the front pew, head down, hands clasped together, trying to avoid eye contact with anyone in the room. Everyone was crying, but I wasn't. I couldn't. Was I supposed to be? Was I supposed to believe that the bucket near the altar with a neatly printed sign "Prayers for the Sanchez family" was really for me? Kathleen had stood up to recite a prayer, one I couldn't remember minutes later, because all I was thinking was: *This isn't my life, this isn't my life, this isn't my life.*

Nevertheless, I was blown away by her kindness. I was amazed by the support from everyone in my life, but Kathleen was different. I could sense her actions were always intentional, strongly rooted in faith, love, and understanding. So I sat there one afternoon, trying to relax in a chair across from her desk, listening to her talk me through the "Well, what now?" question of my life.

She told me about her dad, Steve, who died when she was eight. Sudden. Shocking. Unexpected. A heart attack. I could feel the grief welling inside me as I thought about my little brother Luke. He was ten—already growing up much too fast because of our new reality. I glanced from the floor to Kathleen to the floor again. Over twenty years had passed, and there she was, sitting in front of me with open arms and wisdom I could trust. I had no idea what the next day held in store for me, much less the next year of my life, but Kathleen's calming presence gave me hope that with time, maybe, things would get better.

We talked about the countless grieving obstacles: the different ways our siblings coped, the renewed perspectives we developed, the default "You're so strong" that people loved to tell us. "Of course you are strong," Kathleen said, referring generally to the resilient nature of living with loss. "But you don't have a choice," she said, shaking her head. She had watched her mom raise four daughters under the age of nine—a massive accomplishment and testament to her mom's strength, but a choice . . . no. People didn't realize that being strong wasn't some conscious, valiant endeavor to face your reality; it was a necessity to survive.

She told me about her dad in bits and pieces, like how he was a runner, always keeping his family active with bike rides and spontaneous activities outside. She told me about a song he loved: "She Drives Me Crazy" by Fine Young Cannibals, a song that my dad, too, had blasted many times in our living room while I was growing up. She told me about the glaring realizations of high school. "I remember distinctly when I had lived longer without my dad than with my dad, and that was really hard," she said.

I felt reassured knowing she had been through it all. She remembered thinking, *I need to figure out how I'm going to integrate his memory and impact on me into my life because the time of our memories is getting further and further from my day-to-day reality.* "You don't have a choice," she explained. "Your choice is how am I going to figure this out, not am I going to figure this out?" And that was the biggest question I sought to answer. What was the next step? What was I going to do with my grief, with my life?

Despite the raw exposure of these wounds, Kathleen found high school to be particularly formative for her growth. "I think, for me, the ways I was able to cope early on were faith and service," she said. "It helped me to connect with my dad in some capacity. I thought, *I have to believe in something greater. I have to believe that my dad is in a better place because otherwise, I don't know how I'm going to make sense of this.*'"

I wholeheartedly agreed; I was already becoming more in tune with myself and my faith. I had always been a spiritual person, but loss provoked a certain curiosity about God. While I rejected most ideas about how everything was part of His grand plan, I clung to the idea that my dad was somewhere eternal.

My conversation with Kathleen felt so natural and authentic, a mere exchange of memories and insights from two people who understood each other. There were so many endings and transitions and uncertainties, but the bond we were forming felt like the beginning of something special.

Clicking through a jewelry website, she turned her desktop computer toward me. "Silver or gold?"

She was insistent on buying my mom and me matching necklaces etched with my dad's handwriting. When I resisted, she stubbornly responded with, "Just let me. It helps me. And somewhere down the line, you'll be able to help someone else too." I couldn't imagine ever being capable of helping anyone else, but her words were laced with reassurance. I decided to trust her.

Together we combed through my list of schools. Defeated and uncertain, I found myself impulsively trying to decide. Nothing could change the way I felt about the future, so why not just give up? There was no use in trying to make myself care anymore.

As I hopelessly rambled about schools I had never even wanted to attend, Kathleen listened intently. Call it a sixth sense, call it God, call it her seeing herself in me, but as the bell for fifth period rang and I stood up to leave, she said, "What about Marquette?"

I slung my backpack over my shoulder, pausing for a moment to consider the suggestion. All my life, I had wanted college to take me as far as the horizon would let me, but now, being ten minutes from my family seemed like what my grieving soul needed.

With plans to attend the student Mass at Marquette the following week, I hugged Kathleen and thanked her. I felt deeply connected to her story, and luckily, this conversation was only the beginning of our worlds colliding.

TUESDAY, 9:45 P.M.

We shuffled into the chapel, finding two open seats along the walls. I leafed through the hymnal, glancing up when a new group of students opened the doors and found a seat on the floor. The room was narrow, with just enough space for people to congregate in front of the altar. In my peripheral vision, I could see Kathleen watching me stare at the two boys seated behind a music stand, strumming a few guitar chords together. "That could be you someday," she whispered, nudging me in the shoulder.

I noticed my eyelids falling a bit, but when the Mass began and everyone stood up for the opening song, I decided to open my heart.

I'm not exactly sure what happened in those sixty minutes, but something clicked. I felt more at peace than I had in a long time. The way people huddled together on the heated floor, the priest's sentimental homily from a nearby chair, the Sign of Peace that lingered for several minutes while everyone erupted into hugs and laughter—I was quietly observing everything, trying to rewire my brain to accept this potential new chapter. I could not pinpoint the moment when I released my grasp on my rigid dreams and embraced the change, but when I climbed back into Kathleen's car that night, I said, "Okay, I'm going there."

When we parked in front of my house, what felt like a few minutes of conversation suddenly stretched to an hour. I unbuckled next to her and sat in the running car while we talked about everything. High school problems, college worries, and the grief tearing me in half. We talked about our dads, about our siblings, about the way loss sparked the onset of endless realizations:

- Life is short.
- Time is precious.
- Never go to bed angry.
- Always say "I love you."

All cliché things I had heard every day, but now, these expressions were religious rules to live by.

It was nearing midnight and we both had to be at school the next day, but Kathleen was wholeheartedly present. I thought about the hundreds of other things she could be doing; instead, she was sitting with me, listening and giving from everything in her heart. As I sat in the passenger's seat, glancing between the dim streetlights and her welcoming smile, I could see the two of us were more similar than I had ever realized.

With a Midwestern goodbye (hugging three separate times before actually exiting the car), I entered my house feeling content. I don't believe everything happens for a reason, but I was learning that people certainly come into our lives for specific reasons. In the coming months, each day brought me a little closer to understanding the purpose of my blossoming friendship with Kathleen Cullen. She was the woman I wanted to become when I grew up. I wanted her positivity, her wisdom, and her generosity. I wanted to know that someday, like her, I could use my grief for something good.

Someone—God, our dads, the universe (certainly not coincidence)—had planted her in my path, and a persistent intuition told me she was there to stay.

THE GIFTS OF GRIEF

Kathleen and I effortlessly continued to grow closer. I graduated and left for college, but we were always in touch, sharing with each other and catching up when we had the chance. During breaks, we set aside time to get coffee or arranged days for me to babysit her son, Michael. I confided in her, struggling to articulate how changes upon changes upon changes were complicating my grief. College was filled with decisions and plans to make, people to meet, and places to go. When, if ever, did we get a break? When did I get a break? I could hardly wrap my brain around my dad's absence. How was I supposed to pick a prospective career path when I didn't even know how to get out of bed in the morning?

Despite the numerous transitions of college upsetting my life, Kathleen exuded certainty. When I found myself crawling into bed at 3 p.m. on a Friday or mindlessly staring at a blank homework assignment, she remained a source of infinite hope, a reminder that good things were possible, and they were coming soon.

As our friendship deepened, I quickly realized there was another layer to our story, another person: her mom.

* * *

Gael Cullen and I met a few months later because she was working at a video production company a few blocks from my dorm. Although school left me unmotivated and troubled about my future, my fascination with film continued to resurface in my mind. I had lost interest in too many things to count, but two things stayed the same: I liked to write, and I liked being behind a camera.

On one chilly September afternoon, I arrived at her production company for a tour. While sitting in the lobby, I crossed and uncrossed my legs, anxiously waiting for the time to reach 4 p.m. Kathleen had unknowingly given me so much strength and wisdom since the day we first talked, and I was about to meet the woman who raised her, the woman who lost her husband far too young . . . the woman behind it all.

Gael immediately enveloped me in a hug. I didn't know what I expected her to look like, but with her warm embrace and contagious smile, she was glowing. I could see the resemblance with Kathleen in her face, and I thought, How many of Kathleen's features would I see if her dad were here too?

Trailing at her heels, I followed Gael around the building. She showed me the recording studio, the green room, the editing wing, and the award shelves. We wound through different staircases and hallways until we reached her office. A bright red poster for an annual run in her husband's memory instantly caught my eye: Steve Cullen Healthy Heart Club, Run & Walk.

I made myself comfortable in a chair, and our conversation naturally drifted to the difficulties of grief. After all, loss was the reason I knew her in the first place. My grief had guided me toward a friendship with Kathleen, which brought me to Marquette, which led me to a chair in an office, across from a woman who understood my pain.

Somehow, I knew that everything since my dad's death, everything leading up to that moment, was connected. His passing had set an entire chain of events in motion, purposeful pieces to a puzzle that I was just beginning. Was this how loss would always be? One person's absence sparking a sequence of changes, until my life was completely different than the one I knew? And was this a consequence, a blessing, or just a new reality to accept?

I shifted my weight to one side in the chair, trying to digest this idea. I would have loved to meet Gael under different circumstances, but then again, if my dad and Steve Cullen were still here, would I have been sitting in that chair at all?

I noticed a certain radiance from Gael as she told me about her husband. While she talked about his passing and the lessons she had learned along the way, I could see where Kathleen got her optimism. Words laced with pride, Gael had a graceful way of normalizing the heartache and keeping her husband's memory alive. "You never get over it," she said. "I'll talk about it as much as I want." I admired her conviction.

We live in a world where talking about death makes people uncomfortable. For some reason, verbalizing the pain has become so foreign and unmentionable that most people don't even know where to begin . . . or how to ask. Gael was living proof that even with time, there is no such thing as "getting over" a loss. She wore her grief like a shining battle wound, unafraid of external opinions or expectations, and her unabashed ability to talk about her experience deeply moved me.

I saw so much of my mom in her, and I knew Kathleen and I had yet another thing in common. The source of our strength and growth was our mothers. Many factors contributed to our healing journeys, but I was certain our moms were the ones who taught us, quietly yet fiercely leading by example.

That day was the first of many conversations with Gael to come. Sitting in her office became consistent coffee shop dates (always tea for her), where she gradually told me more about Steve. The unmistakable light in her eyes when she talked about him intrigued me. I wanted to know more, because after all this time, she could recall the memories as if they happened yesterday. Her descriptions of Steve were detailed and lively, compelling me to prod her with more questions each time. With each story, I felt like I was getting a glimpse into the immeasurable impact of Steve's existence.

"Anyone who met Steve never forgot him," Gael said, removing the lid from her paper cup to let the tea cool. The words she used—charismatic, passionate, funny—they were all words I would have used to describe my dad, too.

Gael told me about Steve's dedication as an alderman and his generous heart that always brightened someone's day. She told me about a family friend who had been having a particularly difficult month, and how Steve lovingly surprised her with Neil Diamond concert tickets. In addition to his altruistic personality, he was an inner comedian. "He was always joking around, always teasing," Gael said. Quick with a humorous comeback, Steve was unapologetically himself, bursting with life, leaving an indelible mark on the world.

Saturdays for the Cullen family were usually simple and unstructured, with no scheduled activities, just the organic enjoyment of life outside. Steve turned the entire family on to running, and Gael expressed to me how much she now values the exercise as a time to reflect and clear her head.

I asked her about his passing. I knew she would be comfortable telling me the story; after all, how many times must one recite a life-changing experience until it becomes muscle memory? It hadn't even been one year for me, but I could relay the day my dad died like it was imprinted on my brain. Over time, this is how grief evolves. Slowly, the loss becomes a part of us, a tragedy inseparable from our thoughts and choices. Little by little, we learn how to tell the story, the words finding their way onto our tongues as if they had been there all along.

* * *

One weekend, after finishing the Milwaukee Lakefront Marathon, Steve left for a business trip in Cincinnati. He was supposed to return the following Thursday, but when he didn't come home, Gael called the airline, frantically trying to reach Steve. There were shocking words on the other end: Steve had never left.

Gael stood tethered to the landline, calling the hotel while eight-year-old Kathleen and her sister Annie eavesdropped from the stairwell. As Gael told me the story, I knew what was coming, but I could envision—even feel—the depth of shock and disbelief she experienced that day. They found him in his hotel room. At just forty years old, Steve Cullen had suffered a heart attack, a tragedy that presumably struck in his sleep. One moment here, the next moment . . . gone. Although I knew what sudden loss felt like, the story felt inconceivable, stretching my mind over the raw, unanswerable question of why? *One moment of faulty electrical impulses,* I thought, *and it changed everything.*

For Gael, the shock was overwhelming. The burden of grief alongside the responsibility of raising four children left her wondering how she would carry on without her husband. The following days and weeks were a blur, clouded by darkness, confusion, and heartache. Pressure to return to work added another dimension to the struggle. "I couldn't sleep, couldn't focus," she told me. "There were days where I couldn't even remember to brush my teeth—how was I supposed to do my job?" This was how most of the world perceived loss: as if a few weeks were enough time to find our footing and navigate the new normal. As if a few weeks were the limit, a deadline, an expectation. As if grief was temporary.

The following years included every imaginable hurdle as the Cullens faced life without Steve. When Gael's daughters entered elementary school, the piercing reminder of his absence loomed over every school project and homework assignment. She told me about one of Kathleen's fourth-grade projects. The class was working to recreate *TIME* magazine's

Person of the Year cover for Father's Day. While all the kids sketched pictures of their fathers, Kathleen's teacher encouraged her to pick someone else. Gael was appalled, and as she told me the story, I was too. "Someone else," she said, leaning over the table, shaking her head. "She still has a dad!"

Another agonizing reminder of grief and all its implications emerged when her youngest daughter, Colleen, entered first grade. Her teachers had instructed all the students to create a magic wand, where they should write their greatest wishes. Most of Colleen's classmates responded with answers reflective of their age, asking for a dog, a unicorn, a million dollars. But Colleen finished her magic wand and innocently wrote, "If I had one wish, I would bring my Dad back from Heaven." I took a sip of my coffee, and it burned my throat a little. That would be my wish too.

High school for all the girls continued to present numerous difficulties. Every year, flyers for the iconic Father-Daughter Dance were posted on every locker, every bathroom stall, every hallway and empty wall space in the school. It was the promotional centerpiece every February, with the Special Events Committee shouting during lunchtime and announcements to advertise the dance. The Cullen girls quietly walked past the brightly colored posters, left to wonder what could have been.

Gael and I left nothing unsaid. She told me that loss gives us gifts. "It sounds weird," she acknowledged, "but there really are gifts along the way." I could feel a smile creeping onto my face, my head bobbing up and down in agreement. We both lost someone irreplaceable, but the things we found were irreplaceable too. I thought of the people who had entered my life, the places I had been, the perspectives I had gained. How hopeful, to think that even in the wake of death, there were still beautiful moments to be felt and limitless people to meet.

Our coffee dates soon became writing dates, because we both wanted to document the struggles, the lessons, and the gifts of grief in a novel. Little did I know, she was one of those gifts. She was becoming a vital part of my life, another chapter in my story.

* * *

As I sat on Kathleen's couch one morning, holding her three-month-old daughter, Audrey, and watching a few soft light sunrays filter into the living room, several realizations occurred to me. Audrey was sleeping soundly, with her tiny fingers wrapped around my thumb. Kathleen's two-year-old, Michael, was dancing around the room, proudly showing off his orange clownfish hat. I found myself captivated by a photo on the mantel: a picture of Kathleen's parents on their wedding day. Gael had gorgeous brown hair and the same unmistakable, glowing smile. Steve, too, was beaming. The two of them looked so happy, so young, a single snapshot of bliss frozen forever in a frame.

Audrey stirred in my arms. I thought about how unfair it was that Steve would never meet his grandchildren. The photo on the mantel was just a moment in time, one they could never get back. Michael clambered onto the couch, leaned over my arm, and gently kissed his sister on the forehead. "That's so sweet," I told him, internally melting.

I thought about how purposeful it felt to be sitting on the couch with Kathleen's kids, the sunlight almost intentionally illuminating her parents' wedding picture. For so long, I had been searching for definite answers, constantly looking for a solution to the question: Well, what now? But I was missing the point. Like I already knew, life could change at any given moment, all in a matter of seconds. The question spoke for itself. The answer was to live in your now, NOW—to embrace the present and not be stagnant with the unanswerable.

Life is akin to a series of puzzles. Just when one feels unfinished, we gather up the incomplete pieces to put together a new puzzle. Each person we encounter could gift us these pieces—the next adventure, a new goal, an exciting rediscovery about ourselves. This constant redirection is both a consequence and a blessing of loss. Grief causes hundreds of changes, many of them still impossible to understand, but with each transition comes overwhelming growth.

The black and white plans I once made for myself fell short compared to everything I had learned. Kathleen, her family (especially her mom!), their wisdom, our friendship—they were all a part of the journey, and they led me here. Maybe my dad wasn't supposed to die. Maybe Kathleen's dad wasn't supposed to die. But for all I knew, I was supposed to walk into Kathleen's office. I was supposed to meet her mom. I was supposed to write this book.

More clearly than ever before, I knew I was supposed to be here.

A MESSAGE IN MUSIC
"Good Things" by Bodeans

CHAPTER 13

A LIFETIME OF LESSONS

———

Treat everyone like it's their last day on Earth, like it's your last day on Earth, like your days are a measure of all the things you wish you could say to those you love in a lifetime. Love freely and deeply, for life is more fleeting than you think. Seize the love in every moment of your existence because the most beautiful things do not last forever.

—MAY 27, 2019, A LESSON I AM LEARNING

Every new season encroached on my life long before I was ready. First spring, then summer—they elusively elbowed their way into the year, a transition so subtle I could not pinpoint when one month melted into another. Perhaps grief had impaired my perception of time or maybe just prevented me from caring. Either way, I found it difficult to embrace the passing days.

As that first summer unfolded, there was a sequence of holidays for which I felt very much unprepared: my parents' wedding anniversary, my dad's birthday, Father's Day. June and July were marked by a strong foreboding that I could not handle another changing season.

One morning, my mom's childhood friend, Jenni, called from Amesbury, Massachusetts. She had spontaneously booked a flight for our family from Milwaukee to Boston. It was a generous gesture that perfectly encapsulated the person Jenni is, and this trip was a getaway that the five of us desperately needed. Suddenly, we had plans to head to the East Coast and spend some time with Jenni and her two sons.

Jenni is everything you could possibly desire in a best friend. For nearly forty years, she has been intimately involved in my mom's life. Her generosity, blunt humor, and nurturing disposition make her a mixture of a second mom, a cool aunt, and a best friend.

At the end of July, my family stuffed our suitcases and boarded a plane for a two-week trip away from the madness.

During that first week of our vacation near the Atlantic Ocean, I cozied on Jenni's porch each morning, listening to the quiet waves of Amesbury Port and reading a book: The History of Love. As I devoured Nicole Krauss' beautiful story of hope, I annotated the book's margins, corners, and my favorite paragraphs. One quote stood out to me:

"When will you learn that there isn't a word for everything?"[12]

I stared at that sentence for a long time. Grief was contingent upon the nature of words' insufficiencies. Ever since I was a little girl, I had been fascinated with language, but now words fell short of everything they once represented. They seemed incapable of either consolation or explanation. Through journaling, my grieving process had become

---

12   Nicole Krauss, *The History of Love*.

a personal quest to define what I felt. However, these attempts revealed that language can only do so much. No string of sentences could ever truly encapsulate grief's galaxy of emotions. What was this emotion called, of sitting in my pajamas near the ocean, feeling broken yet content in the same breath? How do you describe the feeling of being lonely and simultaneously wanting to be alone? What about the way you can experience someone's presence, despite the layers of sky between Heaven and Earth?

It was true—there wasn't a word for everything.

On the seventh day of our trip, we joined Jenni and her group of friends for a camping expedition on the Saco River, a 136-mile river that winds through the Atlantic Northeast. We rented several dozen canoes, kayaks, rowboats, and inflatable tubes, and packed some provisions for our authentic experience in the wilderness.

The next eight hours of my day included steering the canoe, avoiding rapids, and calmly drifting down the river when the water cooperated. Jenni instructed us to yell, "Saco!" whenever we passed a new group of campers, assuring us that this tradition was an essential part of the experience. While my brothers and I bickered in our tiny canoe, nearly capsizing around every turn, we playfully joined in and screamed, "Sacooooo!" to the strangers on the river. They always echoed the word back, and for eight hours, we could hear people euphorically declaring the name of the river. It was odd, but it was the kind of liberating, nonsensical fun that seemed to embody New Hampshire's state motto: *Live Free or Die.*

Halfway through the excursion, we stopped at a sandbar for a rope swing and some snacks. The babbling river backdropped by evergreen trees and New England mountains was straight off the pages of *National Geographic*. There, Jenni introduced us to one of her best friends, Trish, a tall, upbeat, smiley woman who had encouraged Jenni to book our flight. I knew that Trish was Jenni's best friend on the coast and that her passion for life had directly inspired our trip. What I didn't know was that Trish was dying.

That night, while the group huddled around a campfire, passing out beers and telling stories, I lay in our tent and cried. Our first family vacation without my dad felt so incomplete. A mix of grief and guilt simultaneously clashed in my stomach. Did I deserve to be sad when life was going so well? The dichotomy between the happiest day of my summer and the feeling of intense emptiness was tearing me apart.

Solely by the glow of my phone, I documented my anger and confusion.

I have often wondered what it means to "miss" someone. In other languages, there are different words for its several definitions. A word to describe something that is absent, one for when we are longing for something, one meaning failure to notice, another one for inaccuracy. But in English, there is just that one word. I can't stand that English is bound to a word so careless and insufficient to describe the absence of something so precious and irreplaceable as a person.

—JULY 20, 2018

I distinctly remember my mom unzipping the tent door to lie down next to me. We quietly shared tears for a few minutes before she said, "You know, it's funny, because when someone has a knee surgery or a brain injury or really any physical trauma, people make sure they get lots of rest, eat enough, and recuperate for months at a time. But nobody knows when you're walking around every day with a hole in your heart."

Then she told me that Trish was dying, with two young daughters and less than a year to live, according to her diagnosis. I couldn't help but feel a sense of guilt. I was walled up in my tent, wallowing in my struggles, while Trish was staring death straight in the face and still choosing to smile. That single moment switched something in my brain. Looking at grief through the lens of another's experience suddenly put everything into perspective. Heartbreak was inevitable, but resilience . . . that was a choice.

Putting on a sweatshirt and something that resembled a smile, I emerged from the tent to join the group around the fire. We roasted marshmallows and told ghost stories, laughing over the unspoken awareness that it was Trish's last summer.

HAPPY HOUR

According to Jenni, "Trish showed everyone grace, dignity, poise, perseverance, and the desire to live." Her compelling personality was built upon her love for giving. Trish was an intuitive, thoughtful soul, always cognizant of how to bring joy to those around her. Jenni said, "She knew what made people happy. She just wanted to give memories to everyone."

In May 2016, Trish began experiencing headaches and nausea. She immediately went to the doctor, and in August she was diagnosed with triple negative breast cancer. There was a biopsy on her breast, and she knew it was positive but never told anyone. The annual Saco River expedition was coming up and she didn't want to alter the mood of the trip. With nausea and stabbing headaches, Trish climbed into a canoe with her family, ready to absorb every moment with them. "The Saco River was such a meaningful place for her," Jenni said, knowing how much Trish had relished the memories there.

When she eventually let her friends in on the diagnosis, most of them were optimistic. "We weren't really thinking, *The prognosis is bad*," Jenni said. "We were thinking, *We're gonna beat this.*"

So after a year, when the doctors pronounced her cancer-free in April 2017, Trish and her group of friends took a celebratory trip to Puerto Rico. Surprised and relieved, they were convinced that the struggle was over.

But five months later, the doctors found more cancer in her lymph nodes and her brain.

Despite this setback, Trish clung to life and its goodness. She continued to rise above the chronic pain and debilitating effects of sickness and find the strength to cultivate lasting memories with her family and friends. She went with her family on trips to Maine and Wyoming, boarding planes and creating memories on mountains where she could hardly breathe.

Jenni remembered one night, during a friend's birthday party, when Trish stood on top of a coffee table and lip-synced an entire Pitbull song. She was reenacting a dance from a birthday party a few years ago—Jenni had assigned each friend a song to memorize, and when Trish received "Fireball," she embraced the role to perfection. Back then, she had worn a bald cap, and now, after countless rounds of chemo, as she danced on the coffee table, she wore a bouncy black wig.

She had cancer in her whole spine, but that night she stood tall, held her head high, and proceeded to mimic Pitbull in perfect time with the lyrics. "It was her gift to those twenty ladies," Jenni said. "That was the last memory that a lot of girls had of her, and she wanted everyone's last time seeing her to be something special."

* * *

In the earliest years of their friend group, Jenni and Trish had organized weekly gatherings to catch up and socialize with one another. These Thursday afternoons included parties, book clubs, pumpkin-carving contests, and other activities to keep everyone connected. As families grew, they welcomed new babies by decorating each other's houses or filling friends' fridges with food. "It was a way to have wine, be with our kids, and talk about the woes of motherhood," Jenni said. Each week strengthened the bonds among the twenty families, so they decided to give it a name: Happy Hour. Over the years, Happy Hour became a weekly tradition for parents to socialize, make memories, and watch their children grow up together.

In October 2017, Trish experienced a relapse. The doctors discovered a malignant tumor in her brain, and Trish's medical future was not promising. Determined to cultivate joy for Trish and her family, Jenni immediately took initiative. She organized a Happy Hour to give Trish and her friend group one day to commemorate the previous years of their time together. The next few weeks were consumed by her efforts to make this day perfect. Each night, Jenni sifted through old pictures, designed a photo book, and delegated tasks for the friend group. For the Happy Hour, she hired a photographer, rented a Kona Ice Truck, and planned activities for all the kids. The goal was to bring a little bit of happiness right to Trish's backyard.

The morning of the Happy Hour, Trish was sick. With steroids coursing through her body, she had not gotten out of bed all week; it had only been days since she found out about the tumor. However, in typical Trish fashion, she woke up and put on a smile. "That day, she had no symptoms," Jenni said. "She was beautifully dressed, perfectly poised, like an angel." The sun emerged from the clouds as if it knew the day required its presence. For the next four hours, the families recreated old pictures, shared memories over wine, and played games in honor of the years that brought them together. At the end of the night, they released a Chinese lantern, freeing their hopes and fears into the sky. "It was super emotional," Jenni recalled. "But it was the most beautiful, perfect day."

Trish's continuous battle with cancer fueled her passion for life. Through scans, medications, and two brain surgeries, she upheld a positive attitude for her kids; after the second operation on Christmas Eve, Trish sent Jenni a touching video belting "Don't Stop Believin'" with one of her daughters. She valued time with friends and family and knew what was necessary to ensure that they had healthy, happy memories of her. Her actions were deliberate yet subtle, always guided by her deep love for life.

After my dad's passing, Jenni experienced a restless desire to show support for my family. She was miles away, worried about my mom, and contemplating the possibility of bringing us to the East Coast for a vacation. As this thought circulated through her mind in the following weeks, she articulated her hesitance to Trish, who ultimately became the driving force behind her decision. "If you feel like you need to do that for them, you do it," Trish told her. "You do it all, because that's what matters." Later that week, Jenni booked the trip and surprised my family with a vacation, the vacation that breathed new perspective into my life.

On Ash Wednesday in 2019, Trish decided to join Jenni and her two sons, Henry and Paddy, for their school Mass. She was nauseous and exhausted, but upon entering the church, she assumed her superhuman regality. Despite the cancer ravaging her body, Trish masked her pain with grace and arrived wearing a white shirt, white pants, and a long, white wool coat. During the service, she hugged the boys over and over and over. Together they sang, prayed, even quietly joked with one another.

For Jenni and her sons, that day was nothing less than a gift. It was a testament to Trish's undying strength and determination to leave behind memories of the things that mattered: faith, family, and friendship. Trish knew that Wednesday, March 6, 2019, would be Henry and Paddy's last memory of her. So, dressed as an angel, she ensured that they spent their final moments together in church, celebrating their faith and savoring the present.

"That's just how strong she was for everyone," Jenni said. "She gave that gift to my boys. She knew what gift to give everyone along the way, and for my kids to see her for the last time in church, she made that happen because she knew it was important."

Only ten days later, Jenni found herself perched in a chair at her best friend's bedside. She gave Trish two drawings from her sons, one of which depicted an elaborate, impressive sketch of a bluebird. Never in her life had she seen her son, Henry, draw a bluebird. Beneath the drawing, in squiggly, eleven-year-old handwriting, it said: "Love you."

As the drugs streamed through her body, Trish drifted in and out of consciousness. She was relatively aloof, on the brink of another universe, but Jenni remained at her side, stroking her hand and whispering comforting words into the silence. Suddenly, as if she had been awoken by a gust of energy, Trish opened her eyes wide, sat straight up in her bed, and pointed to the drawing. "Bluebird," she blurted. Jenni remembers the peculiar and incongruous nature of that statement. "It was hilarious, and she wasn't really making sense. It was the strangest thing, but it completely changed my life."

The cancer worsened. Jenni was the only friend Trish allowed to see her in such a vulnerable state. For years, Trish had sheltered her friends and family from the severity of her illness, determined to preserve only the happiest of memories. "She only let people see her at her very best, and that was her choice," Jenni said. "That's how she wanted people to remember her. She only let me in because she knew I could handle her change."

In her final days, Trish hardly had the strength to speak, much less open her eyes. However, she never stopped fighting, even in those depleting hours. Despite the cancer inhibiting her mobility, she reached for Jenni's hand, lifted her heavy eyelids, and whispered, "Take care of my girls." These were the last words she ever said to Jenni.

After her funeral, Jenni felt an indubitable sense of responsibility to take care of Trish's daughters.

This burning desire sent her on the hunt to find the perfect babysitter, give them meaningful mementos, and provide the girls with every ounce of happiness they deserved. Between grief attacks and interludes of peaceful reflection, Jenni began to see bluebirds. They were everywhere, their tiny azure wings darting through her backyard, perching in the neighborhood trees, and flitting past her car. All thoughts about Trish seemed to be accompanied by a not-so-fortuitously timed sighting of a bluebird.

Jenni now has a bird feeder in her backyard, where she often sits to meditate on her thoughts. "I have the most significant bluebird that comes to my house and sits with me when I need her to be there," she told me. On the six-month anniversary of Trish's passing, that same bird settled on a branch for ten minutes while Jenni talked to Trish. Moments like that one symbolize the hidden fragments of comfort that intersperse grief.

* * *

Before she died, Trish always told Jenni, "I never want to be forgotten."

This statement left Jenni ceaselessly searching, questioning how she could properly honor her best friend. She asked herself so many questions: "Is anything good enough? How am I gonna create a legacy?" Jenni said. "I was struggling and struggling and struggling."

After months of contemplation, she and a friend came across an organization that was "made for Trish": Run for

Recovery, a nonprofit organization dedicated to supporting people affected by breast cancer, especially children. "This idea was presented to me when I most needed an answer to my question," Jenni said.

Among the fundraising for summer camps, extracurricular actives, meal support, and child care services, the organization's focus on mental health for children struck Jenni deeply.

"My whole body went numb and my eyes filled with tears. Trish led her life being a soldier for mental health awareness and wellness. She was a life coach, she was a therapist [to each and every one of us], she lived each day with pure intentions, she was an advocate for all children to be healthy-minded and well-rounded, she lived her life to find ways to support her community and support her friendships."

Jenni knew that she had found her perfect tribute: a cause Trish fought for her entire life.

Jenni's tenacity of keeping Trish's memory alive felt like fire, courageous fire. She was blazing with love, ready to help Trish's daughters find an outlet to channel their grief into positive energy.

"For Trish, it was important that her girls lead their lives with passion, be present, take care of themselves mentally, and take care of everyone else . . . that was her message in life. She packed everything in, All the lessons that she needed to teach, each one of her friendships, her family, her children, her husband—she packed it all in, in an abbreviated form, because she knew this was her time. I felt every moment, when I was with her, that I was constantly learning. I didn't know why, but now it is so very clear to me. It is so clear to me why she did everything that

she did, and why she lived every day with such passion. She taught us to live every day. Cancel your plans, be with your kids, do what you need to do, make them the best food, go on that bike ride, plan the trip. Don't do it tomorrow, do it today."

The first memory I have of Trish will always be my last one: the day she drifted down the river in Maine, with a smile plastered across her face and her family wedged into a canoe. She was sick, but you would never know. At the sandbar, her two daughters nestled under her arms, hugging her waist, shielded from their future. Trish was wearing sunglasses, but I didn't have to see her eyes to know that everything inside her was aching with love.

Trish became the lessons she left behind. Leading by example, she nurtured these lessons, groomed them, and became a model of what living a fruitful life means. She gifted her friends and family with memories, the most precious and everlasting ones, to guide them in the journey when she was gone.

Each person's legacy is really just a collection of these types of memories, stories shaped by the people who loved them. Trish might be remembered for her subtle purposefulness, her unadulterated passion, or the time she stood on a table and imitated a convincing Pitbull singing "Fireball." I hardly knew her, but I will always remember her. Trish entrusted the world with instruments of gratitude, of faith, and of optimism; for this, I know that her story will never die.

In every loss lies a lesson, and Trish left behind a lifetime of them.

A MESSAGE IN MUSIC
"Saturn" by Sleeping At Last

PART III

FORWARD

CHAPTER 14

SOÑAR CONTIGO

———

It seems unfair that I have to approach this new part of the journey long before I am ready. But perhaps this new chapter, this beautifully unpredictable path of growth, is exactly how I will discover the person I want to become.

—AUGUST 23, 2018, A LETTER TO MY FATHER

After the first anniversary of my dad's passing, I desperately needed to get away. I wasn't sure where or how, but Neil Peart's story of travel continued to echo in the back of my head. In so many ways, I felt trapped—in my head, in my grief, in my routine of just trying to get through the day.

During spring break, my friend Lizzy and I decided to visit our high school, as many alumni did after graduation. We had both developed a close relationship with most of our teachers, and so after wandering through the school to visit some of them, we stopped to see our former Spanish teacher during his free period. Señor Hurtado was an easy-going, kind-hearted man with Spaniard straightforwardness and a few iconic, self-made witticisms. In high school, Lizzy and I had often spent our lunch hour in his classroom, asking him about life in Spain or playing hangman on his whiteboard. Sometimes we curled up on the carpet and lay on our backpacks to take a nap; one time, Señor Hurtado even turned off all the lights and jokingly tossed us some costume kimonos for blankets.

Walking into his classroom again for the first time since college triggered a wave of nostalgia. Those four years had easily felt like the best years of my life, and I wanted them back. I missed the all-girls education, the closeness with my classmates, the kind of intimacy that only develops when you are stuck together for eight periods a day. I sat down in my former desk at the front of the room, swallowed the nostalgia, and smiled.

When Lizzy and I casually asked Señor Hurtado about his plans for the summer, he told us about his upcoming vacation to Spain, where he would visit his family in Cadiz.

"We're coming to visit you, Señor Hurtado," Lizzy teased. "Just pack us in your suitcase."

He paused for a moment, unhooking his magnetic reading glasses and nonchalantly said, "You can come."

Lizzy and I couldn't decipher whether he was joking or not, so we both just laughed.

"No seriously, you can come. You could stay with my family."

The two of us looked at each other. Lizzy was an inherently adventurous soul, and I was still searching for a reason to be excited about summer. He pulled up a map of the country and pointed to the places where his family would be staying. Then he showed us a few pictures of the southern cities: the colorful cityscape of Málaga and the glowing Mediterranean beaches of Marbella.

Spain was a country we both had always dreamed of visiting, and nothing seemed to be holding us back.

"Also," he added with a wink, "the best leche."

Lizzy and I smiled at each other as he clicked through the Google images of mojitos and sangria. "Yup." Lizzy nodded. "Only the best leche."

We left the classroom that day after telling Señor Hurtado we would find a way to get there.

So we did. I spontaneously dipped into my savings, bought a round-trip ticket to Barcelona, and spent the next few months of my life aching in anticipation.

* * *

At the beginning of July, we landed on the east coast of Spain. As the Balearic Sea and Pyrenees Mountains came into view, the suspense welled up inside me. I remembered a few words from Neil Peart's novel about his travels after tragedy, Ghost Rider:

"The proper function of man is to live, not to exist. I shall not waste my days in trying to prolong them. I shall use my time."[13]

We stepped off the plane, collected our belongings, and exchanged our U.S. dollars for euros. At the airport, we met Irene, who was a friend of Lizzy's older brother and a sweet, millennial-aged woman eager to accommodate us. Our flight had been delayed, slightly altering our plans, but Irene and her family kindly offered their house for our first night in the country. We piled our suitcases into her car and drove about eight miles north to a smaller, quieter Catalonian town, Tiana.

---

13   Neil Peart, *Ghost Rider: Travels on the Healing Road.*

The view in Tiana was stunning. We circled higher and higher through the winding hills and narrow streets until we seemed to be at the peak of the province. Irene's family lived in a quaint apartment complex elevated by the countryside. While wading into the pool just outside their room, we could see the entire city stretching to the ends of the horizon. A few trees and flowering bushes gave us some privacy from the neighboring buildings, and the sunset slowly melted into a pinkish twilight. If contentment were a place, it was there.

After we had finished swimming and showered, we joined Irene and her family on the balcony for dinner. Her parents didn't speak English, so Lizzy and I fumbled our way through the conversation, looking to Irene for translation when we couldn't understand their accents. Her mom had cooked the hallmarks of a Spanish meal: tortilla de patata, some chorizo, and jamón with bread and olive oil. We all drank some Coca-Colas while Irene's stepdad traced the story of his fascination with boating. Their dog, Iru, a black Catalan sheep dog, brushed against our legs underneath the table.

We woke up early the next morning to catch a train from Barcelona to Málaga, where we would stay with Señor Hurtado's sister, Nena. As we kissed Irene's family goodbye, Lizzy and I continued our trip to the South.

When we arrived at the train station, we met Nena and her son, Angel, who walked with us a few blocks back to their apartment. Angel helped with translation, but Nena was easy to understand, and I was excited to challenge myself for the next two days. Angel showed us his childhood room and extensive collection of American CDs, which included every single Taylor Swift album. His shelf reminded me of my dad's massive collection at home, a vault of his all-time favorite albums. Angel proudly flaunted the CDs, eagerly awaiting our response. With obvious ambition in his eyes, he told us his dream was to visit New York City one day.

After another lunch of tortilla de patata, what was supposed to be a brief *siesta* turned into a four-hour recovery nap. The jet lag was catching up to us, but Lizzy and I slipped on some more presentable clothing and took to the streets of downtown Málaga. With Angel's loosely drawn map of the city in hand, we strolled past shops and restaurants, searching for something to eat. The murmur of my favorite language, the smell of freshly cooked jamón, the normative way that 10 p.m. felt more like day and less like night—Spain was calling us to more adventure.

Lizzy and I eventually found ourselves at a restaurant built inside an old bodega bar that was widely known for its vino dulce, or sweet wine. The two of us wandered around through the restaurant for ten minutes, contemplating whether it was customary to seat ourselves. I could sense the smirks from locals as we passed; my blonde hair and camera backpack screamed American tourist. When I mustered the confidence to ask one of the waiters where to sit, he laughed and pointed to the open seats in front of him.

Dinner was a classic bocadillo—a sandwich—with a glass of vino dulce. Lizzy and I people-watched from our table, keeping a tally of the attractive men bustling in and out of the restaurant. After becoming enamored from afar with strangers we would never see again, we left for the Roman Theatre to meet Angel and his boyfriend.

There we sat down and talked with the two of them for several hours. They ordered pizza and fries while teaching us Spanish swears, pairing each one with a flamboyant gesture for context. Lizzy and I could not stop laughing. The night was nearing two in the morning, but I had no awareness of the passing time. Hours were arbitrary in Spain, and I started to notice that everyone there just enjoyed life as it came. Meals commonly lasted three or four hours, continuing long after the food was gone, all by the thread of conversation. I envied their spontaneity and capacity for being in the present.

Later that night, when our stomachs were sore from laughing, all four of us wandered through the plaza looking for a disco. We eventually settled at a small hookah bar and ordered some mojitos. Angel found a foosball table in the corner and challenged us to a game; I couldn't help but think of my dad and his competitive nature. His techniques were ingrained in me from just seven years old. *Stagger your players,* I thought. *Always two hands on the rods.* Lizzy and I claimed our victory before finishing our drinks and heading home.

After another day in Málaga, we caught the 5 a.m. bus to Marbella, a southern Andalusian town near the Strait of Gibraltar. It was a charming city, situated right on the Mediterranean Sea, with welcoming cobbled streets back dropped by mountains and nearby beaches. For this phase of the trip, we had arranged to stay with one of Señor Hurtado's family friends, Rosita.

* * *

I had been itching to meet Rosita because I could sense her excitement through the group WhatsApp message; every response had been garnished with exclamation points and smiley faces. So when she arrived at the bus station to pick us up, I somehow knew exactly who she was.

Rosita was effortlessly hospitable and had already made meals for the day when we got to her apartment. Her dog, Lola, a chunky pug she lovingly referred to as Gordita, greeted us at the door. Rosita's apartment was small but cozy, so much so that I felt as if I belonged already.

Later that day, Lizzy and I laid out our towels on the beach and played a few card games before wading into the waves. I shuffled in until the water reached my neck and then stared toward the infinite horizon. How did time move so slowly and so quickly all at once? The mountains fit flawlessly into the image before my eyes; I took a mental photo and a deep breath. I was on the other side of the world. My dad . . . the other side of the universe . . . somewhere.

We baked under the sun for a few hours, drifting in and out of sleep and quiet conversation. The low rumble of crashing waves, the murmur of nearby toddlers babbling Spanish, a few seagulls, and the spray of saltwater all converged into a sort of peaceful daydream. I recorded three minutes on my phone to capture all those sounds, knowing that one day, I would want to fall asleep to that same feeling.

We caught a bus back to Rosita's apartment, where we showered and got ready for dinner. When I started putting on some fresh clothes, I found my neck completely bare, missing the necklace I always wore: a tiny gold pendant engraved with the words "Guardian Angel." I had received it for my Baptism, but in the months following my dad's death, I never took it off. Through a mix of superstition, intense faith, and absolute desperation, it made me feel closer to him. The necklace went anywhere I did—in the shower, to my graduation, tucked under my soccer jersey during a game.

When I couldn't find it in its usual place, I instantly began to panic, stifling my growing anxiety while tearing apart the bedroom. Although I tried to keep my uneasiness at bay, it was not long until I found myself in a full-blown mania searching for the necklace. Under the bed, in my luggage, on a nightstand, in the shower—*hijo de puta*—where was it? With my suitcase open and clothes strewn all over the floor, I felt tears coming. Grief had made me significantly more absent-minded, but this? How could I not remember where my most precious belonging had gone only a few hours ago?

Rosita wasn't home, but Lizzy and I spent nearly an hour scouring the house for my necklace. When we couldn't find it, I sank into the bed and broke down in frustration. I felt so silly; it was just jewelry, a tiny piece of metal attached to a chain around my neck, but it was also my suit of armor and my connection to wherever he was. Suddenly, I was five years old again, falling into a fit of tears over a dime-sized object that mattered because I told myself it did.

Grief made me feel attached to things. My necklace wasn't the only object that felt so much like the holy grail of my dad's existence. His old T-shirts had become my only acceptable pajamas, and his handwriting was now a permanent tattoo on my ribcage. It seemed that everything he touched, every single inanimate object of his essence—guitar picks, playing cards, books, drumsticks, and old CD's—I had to protect with my life. I had failed, but nevertheless our vacation continued.

That night I had a dream about my dad, the convincing kind that felt so real I believed it when I opened my eyes. "I didn't die," he said, leaning against the doorway in my dorm room, his arms crossed over his favorite blue Superman T-shirt. When I opened my mouth to speak, he had vanished. I woke up sweaty and tearful, trying to calm myself as Lizzy snored softly next to me. For several hours, I tossed and turned in the bed, unable to put my mind at rest.

With Spanish naturally on my brain, I thought about the word "soñar," or "to dream," always attached to the preposition "con," meaning "with." Revelations like this reminded me why I loved language so much, especially this language. In Spanish, there is no dreaming about or dreaming of, only dreaming with—the idea that maybe, when we close our eyes and slip into our subconscious each night, we dream alongside our loved ones.

Spanish gave words a unique sense of power, as it could convey deeply intimate interpretations all with a single three-letter preposition. English was incapable of these subtle yet profound layers of meaning, and I was learning that my search for the right language extended far beyond my native one. I wanted to believe that my dad's appearance was real, not just a figment of scattered memories. So that night, because of a three-letter word, I became convinced that the people we love visit us in dreams.

The following day, Rosita, her boyfriend Juan, and her friend Paco took us out to dinner. We walked around the port, indulged in some ice cream, and then found an outdoor bar for some mojitos. At one point, Rosita and I found ourselves standing together while waiting in line for the bathroom. She asked me about my parents, and I took a deep breath, ready to recite the line I had mentally rehearsed in Spanish several times.

"Mi papá murió el año pasado," I said, slightly self-conscious of my pronunciation. *My dad died last year.* Unlike the pitiful expression I usually received when first telling someone, Rosita's eyes were glossed with empathy. She squeezed my arm and told me that her husband had died a few years earlier from a heart attack.

"Un ataque de corazón?" she asked me. *Heart attack?* I didn't know how to say "cerebral hematoma" in Spanish, so I just gave her a tilted nod and welcomed her hug. The precise details about my experience didn't matter; here we were, two people decades apart in age, with a lifetime of different experiences, standing in a random line for the restroom, in a different country, connecting through a new language: the language of loss.

I felt a tiny skip in my heart that night, the good kind. Feeling content and understood, I could sense a unique relationship developing with Rosita, and I spent the remainder of my time in Marbella trying to memorize every moment with her. *I haven't felt this happy in a long time,* I wrote in my journal.

After just three days with Rosita and her friends, I genuinely felt as close as family. When Lizzy and I packed our luggage and left for the next city, I still hadn't found my necklace. Although I struggled to pry myself away from her house,

I don't think the difficulty was because of the necklace at all; both Lizzy and I had become close with Rosita and leaving felt like an unresolved, indefinite question about whether we would see each other again. Rosita promised me that if she found the pendant she would mail it to me, and I promised myself that one day, I would return to Spain.

* * *

We finished our trip in Castellón de la Plana, a city just outside Valencia, where Lizzy's friend from college lived. Our days there were packed with adventure: idyllic dinners on the beach, brimming bowls of paella, and nights at the disco until sunrise. As quickly as the trip had come, it was over. After twelve days in the country, Lizzy and I shoved some Spanish olive oil into our suitcases and finally boarded a plane back home.

As we took off and the mountains disappeared beneath the clouds, I reflected on the last twelve days of my life. I think to say Spain changed me would be dramatic, but it opened my heart. The trip felt like a miniature puzzle piece to the grand scheme of my life, my first taste of adventure and independence. I had no idea how much I needed freedom like those twelve days to remind me that, when life gives us opportunities, we need to seize them. My impulsive decision to buy a ticket had been born from grief itself; I knew that waiting for the perfect moment to get up and do something about your life was long gone—there wasn't a perfect moment. No number in a bank account or flawlessly orchestrated set of circumstances could change the fact that life was slipping away, day by day. I was tired of waiting for satisfaction, of carefully planning my life around a future that wasn't guaranteed. My dad would have wanted me to take that chance to travel, so I did.

I fell into a trance watching the wispy stratus clouds below. I thought about my necklace, possibly floating somewhere in the Mediterranean Sea, a piece of my dad drifting near the coast of Spain forever. I thought about dreams and sweet wine and Spanish olive oil. I thought about Rosita and the unexpected bond we had formed. Different languages, different stories, but the same connection fueled by heartbreak and understanding. Rosita was my friend, and our experiences had drawn us even closer to each other. This language was unquestionably universal. If I could identify with a woman across the world in an entirely different dialect, I knew I could feel this connection anywhere.

As the airplane drifted through time and space, I wondered where else this language would take me.

A MESSAGE IN MUSIC:
"In My Dreams" by James Morrison

CHAPTER 15

RISING FROM THE RUT

———

Flowers don't grow without a little rain
Can't grow strong without a little pain
Never gonna heal if you've never been bruised
Only know it's worth when it hurts to lose

—AUGUST 9, 2018, AFTERNOON

THOUGHTS IN A LYRICAL VERSE

Coming home for the summer after my freshman year hit hard. I didn't realize how removed college allowed me to be until my first night back at home, where the raw reality of his absence swallowed me. Grief had surfaced in a rollercoaster of ways while I was gone, but most of the time, it was a gentle whisper in the back of my head. Being physically away from home was a slight buffer between two phases of my life. Now, climbing into bed left me a prisoner of my thoughts, with the silence filling every space where he was not.

I would come home from hanging with friends to find all the lights out and the house completely dark; everyone was asleep. I had forgotten what it was like to be enveloped by such an agonizing lack of sound, particularly those of my dad's nocturnal tendencies: playing the drums, watching a documentary in our basement, concocting a midnight snack. Even the sound of his sleep apnea machine softly whirring in the room next to me was irreplaceable.

On the nights I won the battle with insomnia, I started having wildly vivid dreams. Vibrant recollections of my dad danced through my head and for a few brief and beautiful seconds, I would open my eyes and think they were real. His voice felt clearer and closer than it had in a long time. My heart skipped a beat when I heard a car door slam, or a screen door open outside. For milliseconds, I thought that maybe, just maybe, it was him.

What made coming home the most difficult was my crippling inability to create. I felt paralyzed. As suddenly as inspiration had found me in the months following his passing, it was just . . . gone. I had no desire to write, to pick up my guitar, or even to journal. It was as if a vacuum had stolen all my ideas and replaced them with a dark void of apathetic grief.

At first, I blamed the fatigue. I thought the perpetuating routine of my days was depriving me of all my energy. Work, sleep, repeat, a constant wheel spinning for weeks on end. Then I wondered if I was even a creative at all. Maybe all this time, I had been lying to myself about the power of self-expression. I had no desire to write down my thoughts, no interest in learning anything new. The mere thought of creating anything seemed exhausting.

One day, while driving home from work, I was only a few blocks away from my house and suddenly decided to turn around. Speeding toward the cemetery, I gripped the steering wheel and turned the CD to full volume. It was a playlist I made for my mom and copied for myself that was labeled in black sharpie: "When you need hope." Andrea Bocelli's "Fall On Me" reverberated through the speakers, his powerhouse voice leaving a trail of Italian lyrics down the main road.

It had been a while since I'd visited him. One of the trees above his grave had been struck down by a storm. The gravel path was still muddy and uneven, and my car bounced over every pothole. We still had no headstone, just a tiny plaque and some red roses that my mom replaced every week. His grave was situated at the far side of the cemetery, near a fence that separated a large grassy area.

On the other side of that fence, I could see the hill where my dad used to take us sledding. Back then, that hill felt like a mountain of sorts; now, it was just a tiny green bump eternally marked by a memory.

A row of spruce trees along the fence provided slight privacy from the park, with just enough space between the branches to let the sunshine through. There was a dogwood tree at the foot of his grave. I usually spread a blanket underneath the shade and just sat, but this time, I did not get out of the car. It was hard to even look at the overgrown patch of grass beneath the shade. So I just rolled the windows down and cried.

I screamed at him, at God, at myself. I fell into a crying seizure, banging my fists on the steering wheel, kicking the floor, yelling uncontrollably against the wind, demanding proof that he was there. Reclining the car seat, I waited for my blurred vision to subside.

When my voice softened into a series of hoarse sobs, I climbed out of the car and laid a fleece blanket at my usual spot. For a while, I just sat, unsure where to begin. Was I supposed to talk to him? Pray? Cry some more? It had been so long since I was faced so intimately with my reality.

For a long time, I sat. How does one carry the weight of the world?

I finally closed my eyes to absorb the nature of my surroundings. The wind, a soft whisper. A distant echo of kids playing in the park, a jingling dog leash. The feeling of the sun temporarily warming and settling on my skin. Two cardinals caught in a playful song. My own breath, a shaky exchange of inhales and exhales.

My phone lit up with a text from Uncle Brian: Need help writing some lyrics. I only have 2 verses so far, need a chorus and a bridge for guitar, but maybe you'll have some lyrical ideas for verses, bridge or chorus. Attached to his text were his verses:

Ann Marie, don't you cry
With an angel and devil on both sides
You may have lost your parachute in the war
But there's provisions on the desert floor

Jesus, Buddha, Allah, and Rah
Gods of sons, to be sure
So Ann Marie, don't you cry
They'll remember us when we die

These lyrics seemed to epitomize my emotions. There was something beautifully hopeful about my uncle's words, and I wanted to contribute. When I asked him to explain the meaning behind the song, Uncle Brian said, "It's about dealing with grief and difficulty in life, and how there is this dichotomy of light and darkness that floods you at different times, and sometimes even at the same time. But hope and joy are always accessible to us, even in the lowest times, and the love you have for someone you have lost can bring you back from anything."

I was stunned by his eloquent portrayal of grief. This idea that pain and hope can simultaneously overwhelm us in one breath . . . it was so true. Grief was a spectrum of light and darkness, with some days brighter than others and some an unpredictable mixture of it all. With dried tears and a lingering migraine, I drafted my thoughts.

We can run to the Dead Sea
And try to touch the sun
But honey the sweetest love I knew
The words from the maker's tongue

The wind encircled me, rippling through the fresh blades of grass tickling my ankles.

Ann Marie, close your eyes
The full moon is rising
White flag to the skies
This fire is burning

I sprawled out on the blanket, propped on my elbows with these new words in my hands.

The sky turns from smoke to ash
The stars return
And the night goes black
Ann Marie
Rest with me
There is hope in all eternity

Typing these notes on my phone was freeing. I couldn't decide whether they were dismal or promising, but the imagery felt fitting. After reading them over, I realized it was a continuum of hope, a call to embrace the darkness and surrender. I could not control my grief; the night would always return; the fire would continue burning; the loss was forever.

However, in that moment I came to a powerful realization that hope was born from all things infinite. Although living without my dad was going to be a daily battle until the end of time, it was no match for my immeasurable love. The reason for my intense creative rut was not exhaustion or laziness or stubborn writer's block. It was simply because, that summer, I had given myself little time to grieve.

While sitting at the foot of my dad's grave and hugging my knees, I said three words with confidence.

"I love you."

Speaking out loud to him felt good. How long had I been suppressing that phrase? It felt cathartic and sufficient. I slipped on my shoes, folded the blanket, and unlocked the car. With windows rolled all the way down, I blasted James

Taylor's "Fire and Rain" and slung my arm out to touch the wind. Where there was love, there was hope, and wherever there was hope, there was boundless creativity.

A MESSAGE IN MUSIC
"Re: Stacks" by Bon Iver

CHAPTER 16

THE POWER OF EMPATHY

We are just divided by this temporary, intangible barrier that separates life from eternal life. And just because your earthly life ended doesn't mean that the love and relationship should die too.

—JULY 6, 2018, A LETTER TO MY FATHER

The seven of us emerged from the basement, groggily dragging our bodies up the stairs toward the smell of bacon, eggs, and pancakes. With a blanket wrapped around my shoulders, I settled into a dining room chair. The aftermath of a late-night sleepover clung to the bags under my eyes and the frizzy, lopsided bun on my head. Grace's two golden doodles paced between the table and the kitchen, where her dad stood, pouring a new batch of pancake mix onto a sizzling pan. "Did you all sleep well?" he said, laughing a bit to himself. Passing around the orange juice, we all mumbled a dopey "yes."

Grace was a relatively new friend, but I could feel us growing closer. She was easygoing, loyal, and welcoming, and her home magnified each one of those qualities. It didn't take much for me to realize that life in the Kaupp family was always brimming with patience and love. Her dad was happily whisking the eggs, making us breakfast at seven in the morning. I reached down to pet one of her dogs, who nuzzled his head between my knees. When I looked outside to see the cap of a pinkish sun making its way above the horizon, I knew today was going to be a good day.

Mr. Kaupp set a plate of his "secret recipe" pancakes on the table. We thanked him, drenched our stack in maple syrup, devoured several helpings, and scrambled back downstairs to get ready for the most anticipated day of high school: Movie Day. It was the entire school's annual reward for surpassing a fundraiser threshold.

Mr. Kaupp drove us to the theater while we stared out the windows in the backseat, still waking up, our moments of sleepy silence punctuated by predictions about the movie. I was close to falling back asleep to the hum of the car cruising down the highway, until the wind softened and I opened my eyes to see us parked in front of the entrance. Mr. Kaupp unlocked the car and opened the trunk for us to grab our duffel bags, blankets, and pillows. "Thanks for having us and thanks for the ride," I said, smiling.

He gave me an appreciative nod. "You're very welcome," he said, closing the trunk.

Wrapped in a fuzzy blanket, I huddled close to my friends while we neared the doorway and Mr. Kaupp drove away. It was the first time I met him and the last time I ever saw him.

* * *

Nine months later, at the beginning of our junior year of high school, the Kaupps' world turned upside down.

Mr. Kaupp started experiencing significant changes in his mood and overall disposition. Unlike his usual passionate energy, he became extremely lethargic and easily agitated. He had always been incredibly tech-savvy, but at work, he struggled to remember important passwords. When he came home each night, Mr. Kaupp would collapse into bed and instantly fall asleep. His family worried that these changes might be glaring symptoms of depression, but several doctors quickly confirmed that it was something worse.

One September afternoon, while Grace was relaxing at home, she heard what she described to me as her sister's "blood-curdling scream" from upstairs. Grace's mom was on the other end of the phone line, with the hollow words of horrible news. Her parents had gone to the hospital for Mr. Kaupp's MRI, which revealed an inoperable, progressive brain tumor, an indicator of stage four glioblastoma multiforme cancer.

The radiologist did not know the severity and advised her parents to go to the hospital immediately. A few days later, when the results came back, they bore a paralyzing prognosis.

Three months.

At the time, I remember hearing those words through another friend and being unable to process them. I had never been close to tragedy before. I had no experience with loss, much less the grief-before-the-grief of a terminal illness. With no direction, I felt helpless and unequipped with the right words to talk to Grace. Words were supposed to fix things.

Words were supposed to help us make sense of life. From a young age, I had turned to words to ground myself and sort through my emotions, but I soon realized that I could do nothing other than listen and love.

Mr. Kaupp's response perfectly encapsulated the person he was. Although receiving chemotherapy would have extended his life by a year, it also meant a year of immense pain. Mr. Kaupp wanted to experience life to the fullest, in all its authenticity, so he told the doctors that he would not be receiving treatment. He simply wanted to be at home for his last months, surrounded by his family and their dogs.

For three months, Grace watched her dad descend into illness. She continued to come to school, and I could sense that I wasn't the only one in awe of her strength. Day by day, she returned to her seat in the front of our theology class, where I spent most of the period wondering how I could help.

Mr. Kaupp grew weaker, spending most of his waking hours in bed, but even during these dark days, Grace was able to make lasting memories with him. She told me about one special morning, when she cooked pancakes using his "special recipe" and the two of them ate breakfast and then spent the entire day together. There was the memory of when she came home to find her dad asleep, but as she stood over him, he tenderly grabbed her hand before she crawled into bed next to him. There they just lay together, eventually falling asleep like Grace had always done as a kid. Moments like these reflected Mr. Kaupp's steady desire to hold his family close. They were a reminder that in the darkness, there were bursts of light characterized by the simplest and purest representations of love.

During those months, I prayed more than I had in my entire life. Suddenly, I was talking to God all the time: in church, during class, when I couldn't fall asleep at night. And by talking to God, I mean begging. I begged God for a miracle, because this was not right, this was not fair, this was not supposed to happen.

While driving home from a friend's house in early November, I found myself crying loud, angry tears. As I sped over the train tracks beneath a full moon, the traffic lights softened into a colorful blur. I could not comprehend what Grace was going through, but watching it was hurting me to watch her hurt. Please, God. I was almost yelling, desperately asking for His intervention. Please don't take him. Please don't take him. That night I was silent at dinner, aimlessly pushing around the chicken and corn on my plate. My dad must have understood my quietness because he instantly prompted our family with a prayer. "Let's take a moment to thank God for our blessings," he said, "and to say a special prayer for Natalie's friend."

As the cancer worsened, the Kaupps set up a hospice bed in the middle of their living room. Several nurses huddled around his bed, some helping him with daily tasks, others just holding his hand. "It was so eye-opening to see all their love and empathy," Grace later told me. "The fact that someone can come into your own home, not even know the person, and be there when they are most vulnerable . . . it is God's work."

Despite the heart-breaking circumstances, being in this setting sparked awe and curiosity in Grace. The overwhelming compassion she witnessed from her dad's caregivers every day reinforced her interest in nursing. One of the younger women, in particular, stood out to Mr. Kaupp and his family. She was young, effortlessly gentle, calming, and empathetic. When she left the room for a few moments, Mr. Kaupp mustered all his strength and turned toward Grace. "That's what you're going to be. You're going to be the best nurse," he said. Hearing this story from Grace gave me chills. With overpowering certainty, he somehow knew.

On November 30, 2016, Grace and her family stood around her dad's bedside and prayed with him. As he took his final breath, the song "Jesus Will Meet You There" by Steven Curtis Chapman enveloped the room. Devastating. Numb. Broken— all the words that come with loss—as a man of faith left the Earth on the words of a song sending him to God. And yet, Grace described to me the hope she felt the very same night. "I just remember sitting in my room, looking at pictures, and this calmness came over me. And that was my way of knowing he was in Heaven."

I was in class when we got the text. Our school opened the chapel and encouraged students to go pray, but as I sat hunched over in a pew, hands clasped together, head hanging low toward the floor, I realized I had nothing to say. Or maybe I did, but I didn't know how to say it. What was it like to lose someone? Most people were crying, sobbing into friends' shoulders or accumulating a mountain of tissues in their lap. For some reason, I just felt empty. After three brave months, Grace's dad had begun a new journey somewhere else. I had only met him once, but I knew he was an incredible man, and his death seemed impossible to fathom.

I wrote a note to the Kaupp family on a colored piece of paper, overthinking my every sentence, and put it in the basket near the altar. What was there left to say?

As I stood in line for Mr. Kaupp's wake, examining the hundreds of photos on poster board, I could see Grace across the room. She stood with her mom and three siblings, her eyes and nose rimmed red, a tissue balled in her fist. Why was I nervous? What did people say at these things?

I caught the last few words of the few people in front of me. "I'm sorry for your loss" and "I'm so sorry, sweetie" and "sorry about your dad"—an endless regurgitation of the same phrase. That was the default cliché of condolences, but why? "Sorry" felt like such a frivolous word for death. It almost held a "Have a nice day, good luck" sort of undertone, only dripping in pity. Language confined us to the same word we used for an apology. I saw Mr. Kaupp in his casket, eyes closed, hands folded over his chest. I tried to swallow whatever emotion was rising in my throat.

When I got to Grace, I hugged her for a long time. "I love you so much" was all I said, before moving down the line to embrace her family.

* * *

Mr. Kaupp's funeral was a visual representation of the man and father he was. In a church overflowing with hundreds of people who loved him, the priest, Father Tim, delivered a beautiful service to celebrate his life. My eyes continuously drifted back to Grace, who stood in the front pew, a black dress hanging over her small frame. She listened intently to Father Tim's homily, occasionally dabbing her eyes with a tissue.

As a family friend, Father Tim knew Mr. Kaupp well. He stood behind the lectern to tell the congregation about Mr. Kaupp's undying faith in God, his dedication to his family, and his unparalleled kindness. Despite having a busy schedule running his own advertising business, Mr. Kaupp always ensured he had time in his day for his wife and kids. He always valued Sunday Mass and family dinners, because he knew that at its core, life is about the people you spend it with.

As I listened, it became clear to me that Grace and her family's values were built upon Mr. Kaupp's guiding principles of faith and love. He never left a conversation without saying "I love you" and always kept faith at the forefront of his life. Because he cherished the times his family went to church together, Mr. Kaupp instilled the unique power of believing in something greater in his kids.

I turned to see Mrs. Kaupp sitting in the pew. The day he died, she had written the most beautiful message on their Caring Bridge website, a heartbreaking yet hopeful tribute to her husband. "God is good all the time," she wrote, "all the time God is good." Poised with strength, she sat with her four kids, armed with an astounding amount of faith. "I looked up to my parents' relationship for what I wanted in my future relationship," Grace later told me. "They were such models of faith, love, and kindness."

Subconsciously, I was leaning forward in my seat, caught in the gravitational pull of Father Tim's description of Mr. Kaupp. I drew closer to his words, craving more stories about this man who should've lived decades longer. It just wasn't fair.

When Grace returned to school, I specifically remember thinking: I would never be able to do that. The idea of moving through eight classes a day, for five days a week, right after the most traumatic event in her life, seemed impossible. How did she have the willpower, the strength, to endure each day?

I tried to check in when I could, but even in text messages, I stumbled over my words. I never knew if I was doing enough or too much, or just bothering her with the same few phrases she heard from everyone else. I felt incompetent. Grace was somehow showing up every day, determined to make her dad proud, and I could hardly string together a few sentences. Being on the periphery of such monumental loss left me paralyzed, lacking the tools I thought I needed to be there for my friend. As I wrote words and scratched them a hundred times over, the days dissolved into weeks, then months, and suddenly a new semester. And still, I wondered why God let this happen to Grace and her family.

WHY BAD THINGS HAPPEN TO GOOD PEOPLE

My theology teacher, Mr. Pavlovich, paced across the room, sporting his powder-blue pants and round-framed glasses. We were working through a lesson that dealt with life's most colossal question: why do bad things happen to good people? It was a question that always troubled me and consistently left me wondering whether faith was worth anything at all.

Using Rabbi Harold S. Kushner's book to guide our understanding, he read a quote:

"It becomes much easier to take God seriously as the source of moral values if we don't hold Him responsible for all the unfair things that happen in the world."[14]

Mr. Pavlovich told us that too often, we try to portray God as an all-loving, all-powerful entity with complete control over everything in our lives. "But what if God can't be both all-loving and all-powerful?" he said, still pacing across the room, watching the question sink deep into our minds. "What if . . . maybe . . . He is not all-powerful, but He is just all-loving?"

It somehow all made sense to me. The reason for my frustration with faith was because I believed God to be in control. This idea was an image I grew up with, a concept that most religions associated with their Creator. But if God really was in control, then why did anyone ever die before their time? Why were there natural disasters and car accidents and heart attacks and cancer? This new idea felt more feasible. If we could just release our tight grasp on God as the all-powerful, we didn't have to beg him for concrete answers; instead we could just come to Him for love. I clung to this new idea throughout high school, a perspective that deepened my faith in immeasurable ways.

Until, of course, my faith was challenged again. And this time, it was my dad.

I looked to Grace for understanding, and every time, she was there. We graduated, ended up at the same university, and found ourselves in the same dorm our freshman year. Although she had been on the journey a bit longer than I had, it felt like we were taking on all the college struggles and

---

14   Harold Kushner, *When Bad Things Happen to Good People.*

transitions together. Being away from home, meeting new people, figuring out when to tell our friends—these were only the beginning of a million more difficult milestones to come.

I reached a point in my grieving process where I did not know where to go. I felt lost and out of touch with myself, but I also quite literally struggled to find places to be alone. The constant worry of burdening my friends warped my brain into an isolation mechanism every time I sensed an incoming wave.

Things with Grace were always different. I never felt the guilt around her. I never felt anxious about whether she would rather be somewhere else or if she just wouldn't understand. She understood my pain with every fiber of her being, and when the grief struck me at odd hours of the night, she always came.

One night, after an exhausting attempt to finish my homework, I wandered into the chapel. The tiny room only had a few chairs and a minimal crucifix on the front wall. The lights were usually never on. There were rarely other people in the chapel (especially at 1 a.m.), so with each visit, I claimed it as my special place, the only room on the entire campus where I could be alone with my thoughts, my dad, and sometimes . . . God. Most times, I whispered my thoughts out loud, begging for strength or a sign that things would get better.

With my headphones pressed into my ears and cries muffled in my palms, I was falling apart. Every piece of me was breaking, and I thought I might never resurface from the massive wave that had overtaken my body. I texted Grace with shaky hands. Within minutes, I heard the door open, a few footsteps, and the comforting presence of her arms around me.

We didn't say much because we didn't need to. A thousand words were exchanged in a single glance; Grace was feeling the weight of the world with me. When I finally regained my composure, I opened my eyes to see her turned toward me, big blue eyes and blonde hair, fully attentive to my every move. Even without words, I could feel our friendship evolving.

We shared a casual conversation and a few tears. Grace told me about her journey and the anger she felt in the early stages. The loss of her dad was insurmountable and she was inconsolable; she wanted nothing to do with God. However, she gradually recognized the power of faith. "Even though I was so angry at God," she said, "I have to know there is something after this because it's the only thing that gives me hope. You have to believe in something else otherwise what are you living for?"

COMPASSION'S CALLING

The new semester allowed me to introspect my purpose. In passing, I would often see Grace proudly walking to class in her navy-blue scrubs. She carried a contagious sort of confidence and an aura of resilience, and I always got the sense that she was undoubtedly fulfilling her purpose of becoming a nurse.

When I asked her about this certainty, she said, "I always had this feeling inside me that nursing was what I was being called to do." She told me how her personal story directly influenced her desired specialty. "I know that what I'm being called to do is adult oncology and palliative care." Her words were driven by love, and I could see that this passion was fueled by grief. Her dad knew all along that this was her calling, and here she was, taking every possible measure to heed it. "People who really succeed in that oncology kind of unit are people that have had an experience like mine," she said. "I will walk into every room and see those patients as my dad."

Grace's incredible capacity for empathy is one of her most striking qualities. Even before her dad's passing, her compassion drew me toward a friendship with her. When she told me about her plans to pursue nursing, a few tears escaped her eyes. I reached to hold her hand for a moment. The same things that had broken Grace were also rebuilding her, molding her into the woman she was always meant to become. The falling, the bleeding, the rising—she really had done it all.

Every so often in life, we come across these types of people: the ones who manifest light wherever they go. The ones who attract radiance because they are inexplicably special. The people who are rare to find, easy to love, and impossible to forget.

Although I don't have all the answers, I do know losing someone takes us on an unexpected course, one that is more or less the path we were always meant to take. The people we meet and gravitate to along the way are part of this purpose too, part of this continuously changing story.

During our time on Earth, we collect a variety of lessons along the way, sometimes much earlier in the journey than we would like. After all, the only thing we can do in the face of death is learn. We can learn how to be better, kinder, smarter, stronger, and how to uncover the reason we are here. There are dips, twists, and sometimes highs, but the pain brings us closer to our purpose.

Grace will go on to change and save lives in the future. As her dad told her, I know she will be the best nurse. I know this because her personality aligns perfectly with the career, but mostly because nursing is an art that requires empathy. Loss forged the path for her calling, and Grace wholeheartedly embraced it. She leaned into her heartache, listened to her intuition, and found a way to make her grief good.

"When you know you're being called to do something, it'll take you far," she said, and I thought about how every moment of suffering had transformed the two of us. I was still for searching what I was being called to do, still wondering when I would wake up and feel that same assurance. Her certainty reminded me these things take time. Since we became friends, Grace had become a different person, a change that was both beautiful and promising. She had grown and she still was growing, using her grief and her empathy to become the person she was supposed to be.

A MESSAGE IN MUSIC
"Eye of the Storm" by Ryan Stevenson

CHAPTER 17

A LOVE THAT TRANSCENDS EVERYTHING

———

I am looking for light on even the darkest days. Today I saw you in the sunset on the way home. I could just picture you helping God paint the most beautiful sky, wanting to get the colors just right, the clouds perfectly shaped, the sun the brightest shade of orange. Even though this Easter morning felt a whole lot emptier, my heart aches with love. I miss you today and forever.

—APRIL 1, 2018, A LETTER TO MY FATHER

From a pew a few rows back, I watched my best friend Margot and her family encircle her grandmother's casket, a tangle of skinny brown arms wrapped around each other. Her grandpa, Lolo, leaned forward in his wheelchair, shakily raised a Parkinson's-ridden hand, and traced the edge of the casket. Through silent tears, he steadied his fingers on the traditional Filipino bamboo. Wherever she was, he wanted to be there too.

Everything was eerily familiar. The same priest, the same heavy air, the same murmur of whispers amplified by the church's high ceilings. I didn't belong here, and yet I completely belonged here. I needed to be here for Margot.

Fixated on the reserved pews at the front of the church, I could almost see an apparition of myself from a year earlier. She looked tired—pinkish-gray circles under her eyes, lips pressed together. There were no tears, just the visual rise and fall of her shoulders as she drew in each breath. Poor posture, a blank stare toward the casket, one hand mindlessly twisting the rings on her fingers. I hardly recognized her.

Bringing myself back to reality, I watched Margot and her family break their circle around the casket and settle back in their pews. I couldn't decide whether I felt removed from or personally connected to Margot's loss. Growing up with her Grandma Betty made her death even harder to believe, but my own experience had given me an understanding far beyond words. I felt helpless.

MORE LIKE FAMILY

With sweaty soccer jerseys clinging to our bodies, Margot and I entered her grandparents' apartment: Room 213 of Hawthorne Terrace. Instantly, I found myself in a mass of back-cracking hugs from her entire family.

"The Natster!" Margot's dad greeted me with an energetic high-five. I received a tight embrace around my waist from her little cousin Maya. A kiss on the cheek from her Uncle Bob. A tight squeeze from her Aunt Christy. More hugs from Margot's mom, siblings, cousins, aunts, uncles, and both her grandparents. I felt like I was home.

Since first grade, crashing Margot's family functions had become a regular occurrence for me. The movie nights, birthday parties, and Friday dinners were all part of our friendship. Over the years, as our families grew closer, the line between blood and friendship effortlessly disappeared, and we became inseparable.

As I made my way down the line of family members, breathing in the smell of her Grandma Betty's cooking, I mentally prepared myself for a feast. No matter the occasion, I had learned to always come hungry. The dining room table was crowded with food: cornbread, shrimp, fruit salad, sugar cookies, adobo, pancit, sinigang, siapao, lumpia—lots of Filipino dishes I had never tried before, but the enticing smell of each one had me sold.

Before I could even sit down, everyone was already scooting their chairs a few inches over to make room for us. Grandma Betty was piling a generous amount of spring rolls onto my plate, and Margot's grandpa—Lolo, as they called him—was outstretching his palms to signal a prayer.

While we held hands around their dining room table, Lolo thoughtfully combed through each word, giving thanks for his food, his family, and his wife. Grandma Betty squeezed his hand, an infectious smile spreading over her face to match her cheerful red sweater vest. The two of them locked eyes, and even at thirteen years old, I could see they were madly in love.

After dinner, we sang Margot a lively "Happy Birthday" followed by an even more animated "For She's a Jolly Good Fellow." Her dad mimicked a conductor, leading our Grammy-worthy song with two hands rhythmically moving through the air. I was belting the words, my head tilted toward the ceiling, swaying back and forth with her family in one continuous motion. Memories from my childhood consisted of nights like these, the ones where I felt less like a friend and more like family. Margot blew out the candles on her cake. "Hip hip . . . hooray!" We clapped and cheered. "Hip hip . . . hooray!"

It was a time when life was simple.

COMFORTING COMPANIONSHIP

In my dimly lit kitchen, I collapsed into the arms of Margot's parents. People were pacing throughout my house, a quiet murmur of rustling coats and feet shuffling over creaky wooden floors. A few sniffles and sobs, but mostly silence. Four hours had passed. No one wanted to believe it.

I still felt numb, but when Mr. and Mrs. Dunn cloaked my shaking body with a hug, tears were falling down my face without conscious volition. I could feel the heaviness of disbelief as we shared tears. "We love you so much," Mr. Dunn whispered.

The comfort from Margot and her family carried me through the coming months. Wherever I found myself— bathroom stalls, our school's chapel, hyperventilating on the sideline during a soccer game—Margot had a hand on my shoulder. Before every warmup, she would, unprompted, grab each teammate's wrist and print my dad's initials on the back of their hand.

Many times, I would find a spot before my dad's grave, spread out a blanket, and sit in silence for a while. Margot often joined me, and together, we would cry in between nostalgic conversations about my dad. Sometimes we laughed. Sometimes she brought her ukulele, strumming a few chords when I ran out of words. Sometimes I would wait in my car, tears subsiding when I read her "Be there in 5" text, as she came immediately to hold me and the pieces of me that were falling apart.

At first, I thought Margot was just being Margot. For twelve years, she had been the person to drop anything and everything for her friends. She was the one of the most loyal, sensitive, empathetic people in my life, and my dad's death intensified these qualities with each passing day. I knew this was inherently her—a compassionate, overprotective best friend attuned to my every unprompted silence—but it took me a while to realize she was grieving with me. "I loved him too," she told me one afternoon at his grave, stroking my hair with my head in her lap.

That moment marked my first realization that grief took many forms, sometimes in unexpected ways. While Margot's efforts to console me were instincts, they also were rooted in her own grief. Just as Mr. and Mrs. Dunn had become family to me, my dad had become family to Margot. Although she didn't understand the magnitude of my grief, it felt special to know that she was feeling even a fraction of it with me.

When I received a text that her Grandma Betty had suffered a stroke and her health was rapidly declining, I noticed the same sort of empathy rising in me. I had grown up with her grandparents. Room 213 felt like a second home, a time capsule of simple yet precious memories throughout the years. Margot valued her family above all else, and I knew the thought of losing either of her grandparents was a devastating nightmare.

It didn't seem possible to me. Whenever I visited their apartment, Grandma Betty had always seemed more than healthy. With her youthful glow and contagious smile, she was eager to have guests, whether that meant cooking them a hearty meal or just sitting with her grandkids around a dining room table. There were snacks in her pantry that she bought but never ate, just in case Margot and her cousins came over. Even though she rarely used them, homemade sculptures and painted jewelry boxes from her grandkids covered her desk and the area in front of her mirror. In every respect, Grandma Betty loved her grandchildren; I knew this because, throughout my childhood, I saw this love firsthand, because she had an exceptional way of making me feel like her grandchild, too.

After a few days in the hospital, Grandma Betty suffered another stroke. Margot was away at college, trying to get through each class until she could take the bus home. Her parents often called, asking if she wanted to say anything to her grandma, but it was just too hard to believe. Through sporadic text messages, Margot relayed her grandma's deteriorating health to me, and I could tell things weren't looking good.

When Margot finally arrived at the hospital, the whole family was together. They each received blanket squares, tiny mementos that Grandma Betty touched, little pieces of her they could carry forever.

On February 17, on Margot's sister Ellie's birthday, Grandma Betty died.

Margot and her family were broken. They were without the woman who gave Room 213 of Hawthorne Terrace an almost tangible feeling of light and love.

I felt powerless and frustrated. My experience with loss should have primed me to help others through their journey, right? If pain and I were so familiar, why did it feel like we were meeting for the first time?

BLESSINGS THROUGH GRIEF

Although I wasn't always physically present to experience it firsthand, Lolo's grief was perhaps the hardest reality to accept. Margot described to me his drastic change in disposition. Debilitated under the weight of his grief, he descended deeper and deeper into his sorrow, refusing to eat and struggling to speak. As he retreated into his broken heart, Lolo's physical state worsened.

I hugged my knees next to Margot on the carpet of Room 213, breathing in the emptiness of the living room. Lolo reclined in his favorite chair, wistful brown eyes turned toward the television, with his small feet propped up and his hands in his lap. As he leaned back in the chair, those eyes were a portal to his grieving soul. He didn't have to say anything to tell us that he was aching in unimaginable pain.

The credits of the movie started rolling. I stood up to leave, shrugging into my parka when Lolo whispered something softly and slightly incoherent. "He wants to bless you," Margot said to me.

Shuffling to crouch beside his chair, I bent over while Lolo raised one hand and gently traced a cross on my forehead. It was his customary departing gesture, but those two endearing strokes on my brow reminded me of my dad's nightly ritual. Suddenly, I was nine years old again, tucked into bed when my dad drew the cross between my eyes with his thumb, pairing the motion with a tender "I love you." Lolo's touch was light, the pressure subdued but the intention strong.

I forced myself to smile. The invisible cross carried its weight of a memory, a timeless blessing for safety and happiness.

I buttoned my jacket and gave his hand a warm squeeze. Grief pooled in the deep brown of his eyes and trailed from his finger on my forehead. Loss bred lots of emotions centered around the passage of time—nostalgia for special moments, regret for the past, the burden of new sunrises and sunsets— but Lolo wasn't thinking about the past. He was longing for the future.

Waving and closing the door behind me, I left, not knowing I would never see him again.

* * *

As his health declined, Margot's family spent most nights around his bedside. As another nightmare began, they knew the anguish of a broken heart was irreversible. Seeing Lolo crushed under the weight of his loss was heartbreaking. After only two months of life without Grandma Betty, Margot and her family had to let go of Lolo, too. With his bed set up in his living room, surrounded by his entire family, he died on Easter morning, readily accepting the eternal journey ahead.

So, again, I put on the same black funeral dress, walked into my childhood church, and sat in the same pew for Lolo's funeral.

The weight of the ceremony was heavy, but this time, it included hints of hope. Finally reunited in another universe, Grandma Betty and Lolo had found each other . . . this time, forever.

I had drifted down the aisle, inspecting each one of the pictures on the row of poster boards. The photos reflected a lifetime of adventure. Grandma Betty posing on a pontoon boat with her fishing pole and a puffer fish. Seven-year-old Margot with a fringe of dark brown bangs, eyes wide as she cupped her hands around a hermit crab. Lolo grinning under a pair of sunglasses and a bucket hat. One particular photo caught my attention. Margot's grandparents sat in folding chairs on a white beach in Siesta Key, both peacefully watching the waves. No one else was in the frame, just the sky, water, and two people frozen in a single moment. I wondered what they were saying.

Margot stepped behind the lectern. With her voice fighting against the tears, she read:

"They were so in love," she said with certainty, her voice breaking a bit. "My grandparents epitomized true love. Since the very first Disney movie I watched, I wondered if love at first sight, happily ever after, and true love were real, if I would ever get a glimpse of that magic in real life, if it even existed. My hopes were confirmed through my grandparents."

Margot pushed a few dark strands of hair behind her ears. I remembered how it felt to be in the exact same spot, with a mass of faces concentrated on your every word. Poised over the microphone, she paused, wiped a tear, and continued reading.

"I remember a particular night on the white sand beaches of Siesta Key when the sun was just about to set on the horizon," she continued. I thought of the picture on the poster board, with her grandparents watching the ocean. "The sky was painted in pastel pinks, fiery reds, lavender purples, and sapphire hues. It was a work of art. Everyone around us was mesmerized by the sunset, but my Lolo was looking at my grandma and my grandma at him. It was my earliest memory of seeing true love, of seeing magic."

The entire congregation was leaning forward, absorbing her every word. Our priest sat behind the altar, fixated on my best friend as she eulogized her grandparents.

"I couldn't help but feel a part of something more powerful than anything in the world: a family, a family with purpose to spread kindness and love. When we love each other, we have everything."

Margot concluded her tribute and tiptoed back to her pew. I was proud of her, but I was also devastated for her, for the road ahead was a difficult, infinite journey.

A FAIRYTALE TYPE OF LOVE

Margot's mom and I had always been close. But, suddenly, there was a new window of conversation, an entire new realm of perspectives to explore together. Although I couldn't comprehend the idea of losing both parents within such a short amount of time, Mrs. Dunn and I understood each other on an entirely new level. We shared several conversations about how loss was "transformative" and "puzzling" and just plain "weird." Grief was a macrocosm of unanswered questions, and we found ourselves discussing a few over lunch one day.

Together we marveled over the beauty of holistic memories, the ones that did not represent a specific moment in time, but rather a broader recollection of how our loved ones lived. "Stories are precious treasures to comfort and share, but my parents' daily habits of living are what make their memories breathe life into anything ordinary," she later wrote to me to preface a description of her parents.

She told me about their beautiful love story, which quite honestly could have been a fairytale. Her dad grew up in the Philippines, struggling through starvation and loss during the Japanese occupation. With resilience and faith, he found his way to the United States and became a successful anesthesiologist. With lives that began continents apart, her parents found each other one February evening on a blind date in Wisconsin. "He was homesick, and she had a cold," Mrs. Dunn said. "She soothed his homesickness with stories of her trip to the Philippines, and he treated her cold."

The next day, the two went to church together. "You have to marry me," he told her. Mrs. Dunn was smiling, and I started laughing, admiring his persistence. I could see why Margot described their love as magical. He somehow knew. He knew she was the love of his life. "They believed in a fairytale sort of love," Mrs. Dunn said, "and so it just was."

Mrs. Dunn told me about her childhood, which seemed indicative of the faithful, loving people her parents were. Her reflection triggered memories of what she called "the spirit of commonplace adventure." As a lover of the outdoors, her parents often took the family fishing, boating, or swimming. She told me about the Friday nights when she and her siblings would eagerly wait for their dad to come home from work; they huddled together, faces pressed against the window until they could run to the car and drive to their cabin in northern Wisconsin.

While reminiscing about her favorite memories, she told me about the time they spent outside together. Sometimes she and her mom would wade into the water with a seining net to examine the water creatures below. They named and kept the crawfish, leeches, walking sticks, and salamanders. I thought about Margot's unique ability to distinguish almost any species of bird or fish . . . this was where it came from. Mrs. Dunn reached behind her glasses to wipe the tears as she said, "We explored together, played together, really learned that being with the ones you love gives life meaning and joy."

"Feeling unmoored" is how Mrs. Dunn described her grief. The roaming thoughts, the drifting days, the fresh wounds of loss left her wondering how to rediscover joy and purpose. Her analogy was the explanation I had been looking for all along. I felt like I, too, was wandering. I was unanchored, just moving through the motions of my life.

I blew on my soup while she continued. Since her parents' passing, she was making a conscious effort to begin each day with gratitude. "I mine my day," she said, "seeking blessings and opportunities to give and find love." I knew there were probably a billion stories to tell about her parents; I felt lucky to have witnessed even a small part of their love story.

GRIEF'S GRAVITATIONAL PULL

The Dunn family's experience with loss solidified my understanding of grief and its connective powers. While my relationship with Margot and her family deepened, Mrs. Dunn was forming another special bond with someone who had been in her shoes. She told me about the line at a grocery store that brought them together, a fateful collision of faith, hope, and divine intervention.

Mrs. Dunn had been consistently getting groceries for her parents at Metcalfe's Grocery Store for years and would often find herself in small talk with Tana, one of the women at the register. Although they shared few words, Tana was always engaged, fully attentive to Mrs. Dunn and each customer, a distinctive quality that set her apart from the other workers. As Mrs. Dunn became a regular, returning every week to stock her parents' fridge, the two became acquaintances.

One morning, Mrs. Dunn stood in Tana's line with a heavy heart and a much lighter load of groceries. When she told Tana about her parents' deaths, Tana put down her scanner and walked around the conveyor belt to give Mrs. Dunn a hug. "I lost both my parents, too," she said. Despite the long line of customers behind them, they exchanged a small heart-to-heart and arranged a date to talk over coffee.

As Mrs. Dunn told me about Tana, I could see how beneficial it was for her to form this connection in the early stages of grieving. Loss was common, but losing both parents in such a short amount of time was rare. Her instant bond with Tana confirmed all my speculations that as humans, we gravitate toward understanding. We instinctively identify not just with those who see our pain, but those who feel it too. For when we lose someone, we are empty, and we need a place to share that indescribable void left by our love.

I was curious about this relationship, so Mrs. Dunn introduced me to Tana over breakfast one morning. I had to marvel at the peculiarity of our meeting. There we all sat, decades apart in age and experience, spooning oatmeal and stirring coffee as we talked about our losses. I mostly listened. Tana shared with us stories that shaped her.

After her mom had been diagnosed with dementia, her dad's colon cancer spread, and he passed away shortly after his eighty-fourth birthday. His death seemed to exacerbate her mom's dementia, and in the following year, Tana lost her mom too. I stared into the sprinkles of cinnamon in my bowl of oatmeal. With these stories, I was learning that losing a parent at any age is hard. It's hard when you're young, and it's hard when you've spent a lifetime with them. It became clear to me that loss is less about how much time you spent with the person; nothing can change the reality that one moment they were here and the next they were gone.

Through all these struggles, Tana was recovering from breast cancer, another massive obstacle in itself. She told us about the losses that followed, the death of several more family members that brought her to her knees.

While she traced the journey that brought her to the table across from me, I was intrigued. Our stories were vastly different, and yet so many of her words resonated with me. "I wasn't there to say goodbye," she said, referring to her dad's death. I was nodding, knowing that of all things, this actuality was the hardest to accept. I asked about her tattoos, a colorful butterfly on one arm and a bold heart (half created by a cancer ribbon) on the other. She proudly showed me each one. "I have these tattoos because of how much I loved them," she said, and I peeled back my sleeve to reveal the eighth note on my wrist.

"Me too."

Tana quickly learned to cope in ways I knew too well. Journaling, poetry, prayer—she had even undergone a massive religious transformation following her parents' deaths. She showed me pictures of her house, which had become a living, breathing archive of memories. She had photos, paintings, and a chalkboard prayer wall where she wrote intentions for hundreds of people each night. She had plans of putting her poetry together into a book someday. These creative processes were her special way of keeping her parents' memory alive.

I left that day wondering how time and time again, it was so easy to connect with people amid the grief—people with separate lives, separate stories, all converging into one new chapter of understanding. It seemed that with each new friendship came another brick, another building block to reconstruct my strength.

Mrs. Dunn, Tana, Margot, me—we all were burning with uncontainable love for the people we lost. We didn't need much to keep this love alive—only things like spooning oatmeal, stirring coffee, and sharing stories. For the first time ever, I was confident that grieving makes us more capable than we ever could have imagined.

* * *

Margot's grandparents fostered the type of love that transcends everything. With values rooted in faith, they created a relationship that would surpass all limits, all streams of time, every barrier between the temporal and the eternal. "I see life's three dimensions expand beyond the physical boundaries of reason," Mrs. Dunn said. "Faith extends us into a new realm of being that brings us closer to our loved ones in a real and living sense. Just knowing how their faith carried them through life gives me hope that faith will sustain me too."

I took a moment to digest her statement. Perhaps through faith alone this metaphysical nature of love was possible. Through a belief in something greater, we can connect with the ones we have lost all on the breath of prayer. We can feel their presence; we can invite them to come into our lives and inspire the way we carry ourselves. Most things in life are fleeting, but love is boundless, and faith alone can preserve that love.

When I asked Mrs. Dunn how losing both her parents in a short amount of time had changed her, she said, "Grief is so transformative, and it becomes a part of you. It almost becomes something you wear." The image was strikingly accurate. Without warning, loss strips us of everything we know, but the grief shrouds us like a cloak of reassurance that our pain is valid and very real. Sorrow molds us into an entirely new human being. The constant reflection, the longing (for both the past and the future)—these things become us.

To separate grief from existence would be impossible, for we cannot erase the aftermath of love.

A MESSAGE IN MUSIC
"The Promise" by Tracy Chapman

CHAPTER 18

THE CIRCLE

———

The other night I had the most vivid dream of you. I pray for those moments, that among the thousands of dreams racing through my head at night, you might find your way to the surface of my memory.

—DECEMBER 9, 2018

My dad closed the door behind him and lined up my three brothers and me on his bed. Family meetings were rare, and this one felt curiously serious. At the same time, I sensed an indescribable air of humor. He had a deadpan tone in his voice, the kind he usually reserved for practical jokes veiled in irony.

"I wanted to have a family meeting," he said, cupping his hands together as a preliminary gesture, "because you guys are going to have a new baby brother or sister!" He grinned. We cocked our heads, trying to wrap our doubtful brains around the idea.

My brother Gabe, who had recently received "the talk" in middle school, grimaced while the rest of us stared blankly back at my dad.

"I don't believe you." I laughed, picking at my nails. He was such a bad liar.

"No, I'm serious!" my dad responded defensively. "Why aren't you guys excited? We are going to have a new baby in the family."

Again, blank stares.

"Your mom is at a doctor's appointment right now! She—"

Before he could finish, my mom burst into the bedroom, holding a squirmy, ten-week-old golden retriever puppy. He was wearing a bright red collar and playfully pawing at his face. The four of us froze, waiting for the image to register. I had wanted a dog since I was four; time and time again, my dad had told me no. Was this real?

"Puppy!" I squealed like a four-year-old, and we all crowded around the wriggly yellow ball of fur. Looking up for a second, I saw my parents meet eyes; with excitement and pride stretched across his smile, my dad crossed his arms over his belly-deep laugh.

Still puzzled that we somehow had a dog, I asked my parents why they had made such an impulsive decision, especially since my dad was never keen on owning one. He had recently undergone heart surgery, so we teasingly reasoned he "had a moment of weakness" for this spontaneous decision. My parents laughed along, but then locked eyes again, and my mom said, "We just couldn't stop picturing how happy you guys would be."

* * *

We spent the next several weeks ruminating on a name for the new member of our family. My dad was in favor of those inspired by his favorite movie characters: Indy (Indiana Jones), Obi (Obi-Wan Kenobi), and Doug (the chubby, overly energetic talking dog from the movie *Up*). We jokingly argued that Doug was not a fitting name for our dog unless he became overweight. Somehow, I convinced everyone to settle on the name Leo, which was, in my mind, a shortened version of Leonardo DiCaprio, but I coaxed my dad to accept it in honor of the Argentine soccer player Lionel (Leo) Messi.

As we tried to train him, Leo proved to be a mischievous puppy. He chewed up my dad's favorite shoes, climbed on top of the dining room table, even managed to turn on the stove while leaping up to devour an entire pan of brownies. He persistently pawed our thighs for food during family dinners and escaped to the neighbor's backyard the second we let go of his leash. With the personality of a troublemaker, Leo consistently tested my dad's patience, raising questions for him like Why did we do this?

But even through Leo's troublemaking, we all loved him, including my dad, who showed his affection to our dog more privately. My brothers would come home from school to find my dad sitting in his favorite brown chair, stroking Leo's floppy ears and whispering, "You're my little buddy, aren't you?" At times, I would peer into my parents' room to see my dad secretly cuddling with Leo, who contentedly nuzzled under his arm. When we gathered around the dinner table, my dad covertly fed Leo under the table. Eventually, our family developed these innocent discoveries into a game of sorts: who could catch my dad "loving Leo."

Through the challenges we faced with our new rascal of a puppy, Leo became attached to my dad. Although my dad would have never admitted how much he loved our dog, it was obvious. Leo followed him around the house, waiting for the opportunity to crawl next to my dad and nap under his arm.

Watching my dad slowly embracing the new member of our family almost seemed out of character. He would have never gotten a dog for all the obvious reasons, but he felt a nudge, from somewhere, because this puppy had a purpose.

Little did we know, Leo would become a therapy animal for us in less than two years when tragedy would take its toll on our life.

THE FIRST ANNIVERSARY

After my dad died, Leo knew. For two straight weeks, while people filtered in and out of our house, he did not eat. From the couch, he sat and watched his food pile in the bowl, refusing to respond to treats or the jingling of his leash. When my mom took him on walks, he suddenly adopted a defensive disposition, becoming aggressive toward other dogs in attempts to protect her. At night, he would nuzzle into her shoulder, sprawling out like a human, and lie with her while she slept. He could sense the unsteadiness in our new normal.

In July, on my parents' wedding anniversary, my mom took Leo for a walk to the cemetery as she usually did. Ignoring the bright yellow "No Dogs Allowed" signs, she often brought him with her for the ten-block walk. Leo had grown accustomed to those frequent trips to my dad's grave; when he saw her slipping on shoes and jingling her keys, he always knew exactly where they were going.

On that day, the grief stealthily crept into the air, looming over our house like a brewing storm. I didn't know how to comfort my mom, considering a wedding anniversary was far beyond my personal realm of "firsts." Anniversaries to me were supposed to be joyful celebrations of another year with, not another year without. The first holidays we spent without him were difficult, but this day felt especially poignant. Watching my mom lace up her tennis shoes and snap on Leo's leash for a walk to the cemetery was a visual reminder that she had to endure a celebration of two people on her own.

When she reached his space toward the back of the cemetery, she stood above the pile of soil and prayed. Leo slumped to her side and laid in the grass. After talking to my dad for an hour, my mom recollected herself and stood up to start the walk home. Leo refused to move.

She dragged his leash, but he continued to sit unmoving in the grass, unbothered by her attempts to pull him off the ground. When he finally stood up on all fours and reluctantly followed my mom for a few steps, he turned around and dragged her back toward the same spot. Again, he obstinately lay down beneath the tree, forcing my mom to sit with him.

"Alright," she said under her breath, relinquishing her power to our dog. "I guess there's something I'm supposed to see."

Within minutes, two vibrant cardinals swooped right above my dad's grave. Tears started to form in her eyes.

Hi Paul. Hi Kelly, she thought.

Feeling a deep sense of comfort, she walked home, with Leo trotting happily at her heels.

THE FIRST GREAT LOSS

Through this infinite quest to find purpose, I realized the first eighteen years of my life were bookended by sudden tragedy. The ugliest losses have served as both the precursor to my birth and the catalyst to my adulthood. In some ways, grief changed the meaning of my entrance into the world. Grief invited the two most intense human emotions to culminate in something even bigger on the day I was born. Grief gave me my name.

On a Friday after Thanksgiving in 1998, my mom and her high school friends reunited at a restaurant in Fond du Lac, Wisconsin, to catch up and reminisce about old times. The group was in their mid-twenties, but the restaurant had been the common rendezvous in their college years. My mom's best friend, Kelly, was home from medical school in Iowa, and that night, my mom remembers her being "on top of the world."

Kelly was always a spirited soul, with an unparalleled zest for life and uncaged sense of humor that begged for laughter. Her happiness was infectious, and people were drawn to her ability to have a good time anywhere, with anyone. At times, Kelly was known to become "Melba," her alter ego who was soften-spoken, shy, and awkward, simply to catch people off guard and make them laugh. With a goofy, childish sense of humor and a sweet, sensitive side, Kelly was the epitome of a best friend. This positive energy was always captivating, but that night, my mom could sense something deeper. Kelly was in medical school, on her way to becoming a pediatrician, and had recently started dating someone special. "She was so radiant, so happy, and content with life," my mom said. "It seemed like she was at the peak of her life."

During their meal, Kelly burst into fits of laughter with her friends, as they all shared stories about their lives. When they had finished, the group said their goodbyes and climbed into their cars, with Kelly driving my mom home.

As they wound through streets to drop my mom off, the two found themselves in a meaningful conversation. They had been best friends for nearly a decade and lived together in college. My mom was newly married, and the bigger questions of life surfaced as they talked about their past, the present, the future to come. They had been through multiple stages of life together, from the awkward early-teenage phases to full-blown adulthood. As they pulled into my parents' driveway, they hugged, and Kelly looked at my mom with earnest eyes. "Jill, I'll always be here for you," she said.

With that, they said their "I love you's" and my mom closed the car door, waving goodbye as Kelly drove away.

Early Sunday morning, my mom received a call that woke her from her sleep. It was Kelly's sister, Erin.

"I have some bad news," she said. "Kelly was in an accident. They are testing her brain waves, and it doesn't look good." Kelly had left in the evening to drive back to medical school but faced a deadly collision where a four-lane highway was being converted to two lanes.

With her back against the living room wall, my mom sank to the floor, shaking and in shock. In graduate school, she had worked in a brain injury unit; she had witnessed the consequences of brain damage, and they were life-shattering.

In less than an hour, my mom and dad were on the road to pick up a few friends and head toward Kelly. During the car ride, my mom envisioned her best friend severely brain-damaged, paralyzed, and unable to ever function properly again. When my parents arrived at their friends' house, my mom got a call from Kelly's father. "Don't come," he said, his words piercing the pregnant silence. "Kelly is not going to make it."

Struck by shock, my parents and their friends kept vigil all night for a second, final phone call. Crying, trying to support each other, they struggled to comprehend how life could be so fleeting. "It was our way of coming to terms with it," my mom said. Her best friend, a brilliant and beautiful soul filled with more life than life itself . . . was gone.

One week later, on the day of Kelly's funeral, my mom collected her strength and stood behind the pulpit to eulogize her best friend. She and my dad had spent all week consumed by reflection, wracking their brains for the perfect words. As expected, words were inadequate. They could not relieve the heartache, and they would not replace the emptiness. But my mom took a deep breath and delivered the most beautiful ones to the congregation of Kelly's loved ones.

"So many have been touched by Kelly in so many different ways, it's hard to know where to start," she began. In the following minutes, my mom articulated the love she left behind and her family that was "filled with love, laughter, and music." Like her father, Kelly had been a talented musician and performer, with a flair for playing the piano. "I guess you could describe them as the Fond du Lac version of the Von Trapp family from *The Sound of Music*," she continued.

Throughout the eulogy, my mom recounted stories about Kelly's childlike, comedic personality. Among them was an anecdote from Halloween in college, when Kelly had dressed as a mad scientist, dubbed herself Dr. Heimcrunkle, and even carried around a rat brain to complete the role. "She didn't just act out her character; she became her character," my mom told everyone. At one point, her father had commented that Kelly always "had this kid in her." She loved to make funny faces in pictures and entertain her friends with her "alter ego."

In addition to this humorous personality, Kelly's dream was to become a doctor, not because of the profession's lucrative nature, but because she wanted to help people. Had she been able to finish medical school and heed her calling, Kelly would have touched so many more lives.

"I can picture her in Heaven now," my mom concluded. "I can hear laughter, laughter of an angel. I think that's how she would want us to remember her."

* * *

About two months later, my mom got pregnant with me. The polarity between the loss of Kelly and the blossoming life inside her sparked a new perspective on the world. "The nine months I was carrying you were really an introspective time in my life," she told me. Wherever she went, Kelly was at the forefront of her mind; at the same time, this new chapter of life was filled with hope. One day, she stumbled across a song that perfectly encapsulated the emotions. It was an instrumental piano piece written for the friend of the songwriter who lost his brother in a car accident. Shortly after, the friend's brother and wife had a baby. The description of the back of the CD said:

Life and death, birth and renewal. This is the circle of life that touches each and every one of us as we make our journey through the world. Although one life cannot replace another, this is life's way of showing us that there is no end and no beginning, only a circle that continues to move around us and through us, a circle that continues with us and without us.[15]

My mom felt a special connection to this song. In the coming months of her pregnancy, this cyclical process of life helped her to navigate the highs and lows of grief. One spring morning, while strolling around the neighborhood and reflecting on these changes, Kelly's final words continued to echo in the back of my mom's head.

Jill, I'll always be here for you.

At the exact moment that these words replayed in her mind, my mom looked up and saw a cardinal, singing in almost perfect junction as the memory. She stopped in her tracks. Something felt connected. There was an unmistakable magnetism about this bird; with its timely presence and alluring perch in the tree—my mom suddenly felt closer to Kelly than she had in months. Cardinals historically represented spiritual messengers and other religious associations, and she knew the little red bird dancing above her was undoubtedly a sign.

On October 30, 1999, I was born. Before the doctor even declared my gender, she announced to the entire delivery room, "It's an angel baby!" My parents looked at each other, confused. I had entered the world with the amniotic sack delicately resting on the crown of my head like a halo. As the doctor transferred me to my mom's arms and she held me for the first time, a wide smile spread across my dad's face.

"Do you want to name her after Kelly?" he asked. With indefinable emotions coursing through her blood, my mom

---

15   Spielberg, Robin. Spa Piano. 2006, compact disc.

agreed. Natalie Kathryn, they decided, assuming her middle name.

I, of course, do not remember that day, but each time I hear the story, I know she was there. A woman who touched another's life so deeply that her memory will forever be preserved by my name. A person who could have changed the world. A best friend and a guardian angel.

My mom sends Kelly's parents flowers each year on her birthday and has not missed a year in over two decades. She and her group of high school friends started a tradition called "Secret Angel" in which they would pick names and buy one another gifts or cards throughout the year. Cardinals have since become an anchor of spirituality, an emblem of connection with those she has lost along the way.

Although I never met Kelly, I feel blessed to carry these stories with me. I am still searching for my purpose, and maybe I always will be, but part of me feels that part of my purpose is to carry them. To keep these loved ones alive through memories, even if they aren't my memories. This is life, this is the circle of life, and this is how we move through its stages. We experience, we learn, we share. The unending cycle of adversity and hope carries the rebirth of stories, so that we might never forget those we have lost. With each new life, lost life, and every stage in between, our potential to remember is boundless.

A MESSAGE IN MUSIC
"Everglow" by Coldplay

CHAPTER 19

DAD ROCK RADIO

———

It's crazy to think you'll never see me move into this new chapter of my life. You'll never meet the people to come and I now must bring you to life through stories, but this time I'll be starting from the beginning. But I promise that every person that enters my life from here on out will come to know the incredible dad you were.

—AUGUST 26, 2018, A LETTER TO MY FATHER

Meeting Jenn Walter my freshman year of college was anything but a coincidence.

Our paths crossed when I sought out a grief group on campus. Aside from the stereotypical connotations the words "grief group" held, I had few expectations. Honestly, I joined because my mom told me to. Well, delicately suggested in the way concerned moms do when they know what is best for you.

During the first meeting, about ten of us huddled around a plastic card table, nervously rehashing our stories to each other. It was the first time I had ever told anyone my story from start to finish aloud. As I spoke, some of the details felt jumbled, blurring together in an anxious attempt to form a coherent, chronological account. I didn't cry. Describing the details leading up to my dad's death still didn't feel real, but I supposed that's why I'd come: to help myself process the harsh truths of my trauma.

Each week, we told our stories a little differently, sometimes in a long-winded tear-jerking description, and other times a blunt, single sentence. There were so many ways to tell a single story; we were all trying to figure out the best way to piece together our own.

While we passed around donuts, tissues, and the routine "happies and crappies" of the week, our group leader, Ann, was adamant that our biweekly meetings were not going to feel like group therapy. She had a lighthearted, facetious sense of humor, quickly reminding us we were entitled to grieve however we pleased. Together we ranted, cried, and even cracked morbid jokes simply because we had the right to. At the end of the day, we were just a bunch of average college kids looking for a sense of community to normalize our experiences and feel less alone.

When every other Friday morning rolled around, Jenn was usually quiet—not in a timid, uncomfortable sort of way, but she maintained a more reserved, attentive disposition when we took turns talking. She always shared her thoughts, but her humility kept her from telling us the most momentous details of her life, like the fact that she was producing an entire radio show in memory of her dad.

In meetings, our discussions centered around our coping mechanisms and feelings of the week, scattered with the occasional nostalgic story about our loved ones. So when a local news channel aired a story about Jenn and Dad Rock Radio, I was shocked by the startling parallels in our experiences.

THE OTHER MUSICIAN

Just like my dad, Steve Walter was a self-taught drummer and guitarist. He was a music enthusiast, often spending his weekend nights jamming with friends in the living room or crafting a guitar riff while Jenn's mom sang. Steve was an engineer, but a creative at heart. He had an entire section of their basement dedicated to both his personal and professional engineering projects; he often tinkered with old electronics and toyed around with spare parts of computers. Steve had a knack for drawing as well. Before becoming an engineer, he had high school dreams of becoming an artist. Always doodling, he accumulated a massive collection of detailed cartoons and drawings over the years. Looking back on her childhood, Jenn said to me, "he took all the aspects of design and was able to make art out of things and apply them to engineering, which made him successful. I think he was always an artist deep down."

Steve's constant creativity fueled his excitement for life, but above all, his passion was music.

While I watched the segment on TV, I was astonished by how much I didn't know about Jenn's story. Every other week, we sat only a few feet away from each other in grief group, completely unaware of the striking similarities between our fathers.

In March 2018, during her junior year of college, Jenn left for a study abroad program in Germany. She passed through airport security, turned around to wave goodbye to her parents, and unknowingly saw her dad for the very last time.

Only a few weeks into her trip, while staying at a hostel in Hamburg, Jenn received a frantic call around midnight from her sisters. "Go into the hall," they said. "Something terrible happened." She recalled the words tumbling out of her sisters' mouths from the other side of the phone, thousands of miles away, a different time zone, a different life.

After finishing a business trip in Las Vegas, Jenn's dad had taken an extra day to spend time with a friend there, but his arm went numb while they were in a casino. He was rushed to the hospital via ambulance due to a heart aneurysm, and the doctors ordered him into emergency surgery. As Jenn desperately tried to reach her dad's phone, she found herself leaving a tearful voicemail, saying, "Call me when you get the chance." She received one last text from him before he was rushed into the operating room:

I love you, Jennifer.

During that night in Germany, Jenn was certain that the surgery would be successful, peacefully unaware of how drastically her life would change in the coming hours. "That night I slept like a baby, trusting that everything would be back to normal," she later wrote. "It was the last night I slept soundly for almost a year."[16]

* * *

When Jenn lost her dad, she, too, turned to music. After returning home to Michigan for the funeral, her first instinct was to make a playlist. I thought about my first long, sleepless

---

16 "The day the music lived," Marquette University, Jennifer Walter, accessed January 9, 2020.

night, where my brother Dominic and I had spent hours creating our own playlist for our dad. Her reasoning mirrored the thoughts in my head. "Whenever I listened to my Dad's music, I felt less alone," she said.[17] "It brought back memories of hearing him play the same few songs on his guitar over and over. I recalled family road trips and lazy Sunday evenings with Dad blasting his favorite tunes from the computer. I remembered moments of discovery and rediscovery, like when I started listening to Paul Simon in high school and realized I knew a fair amount of songs already, thanks to my dad."[18]

Like Jenn, music was wrapped up in all the intricacies of my grief. I hardly valued my dad's favorite songs until after his death, when I realized how much they had shaped my childhood and relationship with him. Jenn and I were both clinging to music, trying to honor our fathers through their precious collections of songs.

With several more weeks left in her study abroad program, Jenn went back to Europe. She had little time to grieve, little time to let herself feel the pain at all. "When Dad passed away, I anticipated sadness. I anticipated emptiness, guilt, and the bottomless pit of what-ifs," she said. "But I didn't know how deeply lonely I would feel."[19]

As she finished her remaining days abroad, Jenn often found herself looking for places to simply sit, places to process, to think, to feel. While the reality of her dad's death began to sink in, the rolling hills of Germany gave her the space to

---

17   Ibid.
18   Ibid.
19   Ibid.

experience grief in whatever form it came. Although I was not halfway across the world with my pain, I had also found solitary spots to feel the weight of my loss. His grave, an empty soccer field, and long car rides by myself had become necessary places to contemplate my thoughts.

When Jenn came back to campus, she returned to work at the university's student-run radio station. Much like my dad had invested himself in my passions, her dad had always been one of her biggest supporters. He texted her before each airing and tuned in to Jenn's every moment on the radio. So when she began thinking about producing a new radio show, she knew she had her dad's support.

At the beginning of her senior year, Jenn and her sister Natalie created *Dad Rock Radio* to reminisce about family stories and play their dad's favorite songs. Every Friday, the two of them crafted a playlist and shared special memories about their dad on the air. "I wasn't afraid to make my grief public," Jenn said. "After all, it was the only way I could properly process what I was going through. I wanted to show my peers that it was okay not to be okay."[20]

Her show was born solely out of a desire to process her pain and keep her dad's memory alive, but *Dad Rock Radio* quickly gained momentum. After piquing the interest of the community, the show earned two awards from the Wisconsin Broadcaster's Association. Meanwhile, Jenn never mentioned this success in grief group and spent the hour attentive to everyone else.

Listeners were fascinated by Jenn and her sister's openness to sharing their story. Their vulnerability and creativity

---

20 Ibid.

driven by grief was not only unique, but powerful. People wanted more.

Just as quickly as it had started, *Dad Rock Radio* became a place for the two sisters to interview others about their experience with loss. "There was a part of me that wanted this show to transcend my own story," Jenn said. "I craved a space to talk about my grief and connect with those who had experienced a deep loss and even those who hadn't. What better way to do that than create my own space through music and storytelling?"

In my entire year of grieving, I had never felt such a strong connection to someone else's experience. Jenn and I were merely acquaintances, but I knew our stories aligned for a purpose.

A few days later, I sent her a long (four or five scrolls kind of long) text message explaining why her story resonated with me so much. I shared that my dad had been an avid musician as well, and how I had also made a playlist to commemorate all his favorite songs. Like me, Jenn was shocked by our similarities and graciously asked me to be a guest on the radio show.

* * *

Later that month, only weeks after the one-year anniversary of my dad's death, I had my first experience "on the air." Jenn and I sat next to each other in the recording room, hovering anxiously over the microphones, waiting for our cue to start. I was nervous. I had never talked openly about my dad with such a large audience of people I didn't know and couldn't see. While I scribbled my last-minute thoughts onto a crumpled piece of scrap paper, Jenn took the lead as "Landslide" by Fleetwood Mac faded out.

"Welcome to Dad Rock Radio. I'm Jenn!" Her lively introduction floated through the microphone.

Jenn had a voice and personality built for the radio. She went on to mention the "album of the week," recap the last episode, and introduce me as the guest for the day. I felt unprepared to verbalize my thoughts and tell my story, but as Jenn started our conversation, I relaxed into my seat.

Over the next two hours, I shared as much as I could: my dad's love of music, the story of how I lost him, the beginning of my new creative journey. I surprised myself with how easily the words came out, but when someone finally understands your story, you can't seem to stop talking.

Through heartfelt sentiments and funny anecdotes, Jenn and I breezed through the episode. The conversation was effortless, guided by our honest thoughts and enthusiasm about our connection. Jenn brought out truths in me that I had pushed to the back pocket of my brain for months; we acknowledged "grief attacks," as I called them, the way physical pain and psychological pain inevitably clash together. "You almost feel the physical pain because your body is so desperately trying to comprehend what's going on," Jenn reasoned. Touching on panic attacks and mental breakdowns, she had the ability to normalize what we were going through, and it was comforting. I could feel my grief taking a new shape, embracing these perspectives that most people were too afraid to address.

I was loosening up, liberating myself as the words spilled into the microphone. Any previous inhibitions had disappeared, because Jenn's presence alone put me at ease. As we closed the episode, I finally understood why she spoke to a bunch of random people about her grief. Talking with someone else on a platform dedicated to loss encouraged me to delve deeper into my experience and explore what I was feeling in a much different way. It was relief, a promise for new opportunities, an alleviation of loneliness and confusion.

Jenn and I grew closer after that. She graduated and found a full-time job, but we still found time on weekends to get ice cream or hang out in her apartment. I saw my dad in her dad. I saw myself in her. And the more time we spent together, the more inspired I felt to create. Jenn was always making something, and together we challenged each other's artistic limits. We discussed plans of developing a new podcast dedicated to exploring music, and often shared excerpts of writing with each other. As one of my strongest sources of support, Jenn pushed me to finish this book. She reminded me to grieve, to put my feelings on paper, to document my experience because it was the only way we knew.

Jenn restored parts of me that were broken, lost, and empty. She gave me hope. She gave me strength. But, more importantly, she gave me a friendship that reminded me to breathe again.

A MESSAGE IN MUSIC
"Someday, Someway" by Marshall Crenshaw

CHAPTER 20

SOLITUDE

———

There was a time
when life was kind
and I was so naive
to think that life
would give us time
before you had to leave.

—JUNE 10, 2018, A LYRICAL VERSE FOR MY FATHER

As the remaining weeks of high school dragged on, I found it difficult to find meaning in any of my classes. My dad and his absence occupied my thoughts most hours of the day, and I had completely lost my appetite for learning. When I couldn't focus, or felt the twinge of grief growing inside me, I would usually dismiss myself to a quiet place and welcome the tears.

One afternoon, I could feel the pain surfacing, but this time in a much different way. The swelling anxiety in my stomach wasn't stifled under the pressure to stay at my desk until the bell rang; instead, a fresh strain of emotion was rising in my chest, a compelling invitation to leave.

That day we had a substitute teacher, so I quietly zipped my backpack, snuck out the door, and freed myself to the parking lot.

When I got to the cemetery, I lost control. My world was spinning, and my vision was blurring, in the same way that my senses failed me on the day I learned he was gone. Several angry screams escaped my throat before I was at war with the world. I never knew emotions could feel so much like bleeding.

The storm eventually settled, and my vision cleared. Through swollen eyes, I looked up to see the circle of dogwood trees around me. They were in full bloom, with white flowers falling softly onto the hood of my car. The sun was gleaming through the branches, and the wind breathed a soft whisper into my cracked windows. The flurry of white flowers was a sort of summery snow. I opened the door to go sit on the grass, as I usually did when I felt lost.

There was a small tree behind me, hanging over his resting place, protectively shading the area from the rest of the cemetery. I reclined on the grass and just focused on breathing. The sky was a quintessential tint of blue, with puffy white clouds floating above me. A monarch butterfly flitted through the air, almost intentionally swooping above his grave. My hands were folded neatly over my chest, and I morbidly imagined my family a few months earlier, gathered around this very spot to lower his body into the ground. At what point in eternal life does your soul look down instead of up?

I lay there for a few minutes, accepting the natural flow of thought and recovering from whatever hurricane of emotions had just taken over my body. Looking through the tree branches dividing the sky into a mosaic of blues and whites,

I felt the need to be higher . . . closer to Heaven, closer to my dad. As a strange sense of peace came over me, I decided to climb the tree.

It wasn't a steady tree, maybe twenty years old, with a few guiding branches hidden among the flimsy ones. I grabbed the thickest bough, fixed my feet on the trunk, and pulled myself up. Swinging my legs over the branches and leaning back toward the fork of the tree, I slipped into a reverie of deep thought.

The tiny white flowers continued to shower his grave with each gust of wind. Being elevated above the cemetery provided a strangely beautiful perspective that almost made me forget where I was. Was this what my dad saw? I looked down again and envisioned the congregation of family and friends below, hugging, crying, praying. I saw myself with my head between my knees and a guitar at my side. There was my uncle scribbling some lyrics in a notebook and cracking open a beer. My mom, with our dog, whispering some words of gratitude and scattering a few roses. I thought of all the people who had come to this very spot.

The butterfly returned, circling the tree and settling onto the grass below. Her vibrant orange wings were unmistakable against the uneven patch of greenish-brown, and I found myself mesmerized by her beauty. I thought she might fly away when the wind rippled through the trees, but she stayed. With wings poised on her body, antennae gently scanning the air, the butterfly perched on a blade of grass. I visualized my worries written on those wings—all my struggles to adapt and reluctance to change—I visualized those fears running through her delicate black veins, one and the same with those fiery orange wings.

I was evolving, and I had been for months. While these changes were invisible on the surface, my entire soul was taking another shape, metamorphosing into something unrecognizable. With fresh wings, slightly weak and still developing, I had been forced to leave my little cocoon of comfort, taking flight into a life I never asked for. Although I didn't have a choice, I was steadily emerging from the familiar into the foreign, growing into myself, gradually learning to embrace the transformation.

The butterfly rose off the ground and soared toward the sun until it was just an orange speck in the sky.

Bringing myself out of deep thought, I felt slightly childish still perched in the wobbly tree; plus, if anyone saw me, I certainly didn't have an explanation. "Hey, eighteen-year-old girl, what are you doing wedged in that tiny tree?" was not a question I wanted to answer, so I half-jumped, half-fell out of the tree, scraping my knee a bit, and headed home.

On the way back, I passed Cosmos, a Greek family-owned restaurant that served "the best burgers of all time," according to my dad. With the car moving forward and my eyes still glued to the restaurant, I impulsively pulled a U-Turn and stopped inside.

The woman at the counter, Tina, immediately recognized me and greeted me at the door with a hug. My dad had spent hours in Cosmos, socializing with the workers, talking soccer with her nephews. He always raved about their food, ordering his usual (a cheeseburger and some Greek fries) and eventually turning my entire family on to the restaurant; he was easily their most enthusiastic customer.

Tina and I had never really spoken before, aside from the few times I tagged along with my dad to get his coveted burger. However, there was no awkward transition from our greeting to conversation. After proudly showing me a few of her daughter's prom pictures, we moved into a deeper discussion. She shared with me that she had lost her dad at a very young age, and it changed her in every way.

Tina was convincingly certain that grief was about using your pain in every situation to make your loved one proud. "They are always with you, you know," she said, touching my arm. "See, we can talk to him right now." Looking toward the ceiling and cupping one hand around her mouth, she declared, "Hey Paul! I'm hanging out down here with your daughter!" Grateful I listened to my gut and decided to make a pit stop at Cosmos, I ordered my dad's favorite burger (later labeled permanently on the menu as "Paul's Fav") along with some Greek fries.

I left with a massive smile on my face, feeling full in both stomach and spirit.

GROWING UP TOO SOON

When I started talking to Joseph Chirichigno, one of the first things he said to me was "I have definitely become more comfortable spending time alone."

That single sentence resonated with me because of its truth. Loss had a powerful way of making me feel drawn to solitude. I had never been someone who particularly enjoyed being alone; I occupied most of my time with friends and considered myself a tireless extrovert. However, after March 9, 2018, I began to crave time alone, to reflect and recharge. This time with my thoughts became my most valuable possession. Grief had changed me in a multitude of ways, and because I was an entirely new human being, I needed time to relearn who I was.

Joseph and I became acquaintances through my university's grief group. We had never met because he graduated a few years before I got to college, but when I reached out in a group chat about my experience, he was more than willing to speak with me. Although he lived in Texas, the instant fluidity of our conversations convinced me that we were similar in ways beyond our losses. Joseph seemed to be a writer at heart, with an adventurous philosophy on life and a deep passion for music. The distance between us was startling proof that this common language of loss could stretch between strangers anywhere.

I was impressed by how accurately he could articulate his experience. Joseph blatantly acknowledged the details of grief that often get lost in the bigger picture. He elaborated on the exact emotions, the changes he had undergone, and the way a loss can swallow you whole. As he shared his thoughts with me, five years after losing his mom, the pain was palpable, evidence that although he was changed, the pain was still very much there.

* * *

Danette Chirichigno was an outgoing, charismatic woman with a diverse circle of friends. "She got along with just about anyone," Joseph told me. In addition to her abundant social life, Danette valued spending time with her family. Joseph's childhood was characterized by various activities with his mom: watching home improvement shows on HGTV, listening to Michael Bublé, shopping, and attending sports events together.

When he was in third grade, she was diagnosed with breast cancer. "I somehow knew that it was really not good at all," he said. "It was a school day, and I remember just kind of ruminating on it while everyone else around me was really happy. It felt like I was in a completely different world." I pictured a little boy in a classroom of chaos, sitting in his chair and processing this truth, already growing up too soon.

Although Danette lovingly sheltered her two sons from the severity of her condition, anxiety about losing his mom affected Joseph early on. "I would have nightmares when I was a kid of my mom passing away," he told me. "It was just this paranoia of something bad happening to a family member."

For six years, Danette was sick, but she disguised most of the pain. "She was so tough," Joseph reflected. "I don't think I really understood how sick she was. Looking back on it now, there were a lot of moments where it was really bad and I didn't have a single clue about it, mostly because of the kind of person that she was." Immediately, I thought of Kim and Trish, two other women who hid most of their sickness from their kids. To get up every morning and be a parent, even with cancer wearing away at their bodies: that took a different kind of strength.

During Joseph's freshman year of high school, his mom went into remission. However, just when the six-year journey deceitfully seemed to end, the cancer returned in her bones and quickly spread to her lungs. As Joseph recalled, "That is when things really started to get bad." With cancer overwhelming her body, Danette still found the strength to make memories with Joseph, her oldest son, Jack, and husband John. They traveled to Italy, went out to dinner around Houston, watched movies (Joseph admitted to the occasional chick flick), listened to music, and took in life together.

"It was the very first day of 2015 when my life was shattered," Joseph eventually wrote to me in an email, finding that the words came most easily through writing. In the early hours of the morning, his dad called him to say that his mom was in the hospital, feeling progressively worse. Joseph expected the usual: a few tests and predictable results before they sent her home.

"It is not good," his dad said, and Joseph knew exactly what that meant. He had spent his entire childhood and adolescence fearing his mom's death, even in his dreams. "But through all that preparation I was still utterly stunned and destroyed," he wrote. I knew there was no way to truly prepare for loss, even if sickness had foreshadowed someone's death for years. There's no way to plan for your perspectives, reactions, or coping mechanisms, because when you first experience loss, it's nothing like you thought it would be.

Joseph's dad told him she had around a week to live. When the two hung up, Joseph fell silent. "They say death brings about strange reactions," he wrote. "For some odd reason, I got dressed and went running. It wasn't my typical running though; it was running with anger and heartbreak. I don't think I've ever run that hard in my life, nor do I think I ever will again." His attention to the peculiar ways we react to loss reminded me of my brother Dominic sprinting out of the hospital. He had disappeared around the corner, his screams carrying him far beyond the stuffy waiting room of our reality. In a less literal way, my instinct had been to run too—to escape the person I used to be and sprint toward this new person I was still becoming.

Spending the next four days in the hospital, Joseph hovered over his mom's bedside. "I have never liked hospitals," Joseph recalled. "I hate the smell, the fluorescent lights, the coldness, the beeping, the sickness." His mom was hardly herself, rarely making sense between bursts of consciousness, as the medication coursed through her body. Joseph was falling apart as he watched his mom approach death. However, Danette never let go of her indestructible faith. "She continually said she knew she was going to Heaven," he said.

During his mom's final days, Joseph craved normalcy. Roaming from the hospital to his house, he would often leave to pretend that her sickness wasn't real. Being physically removed from her room was his way of trying to prevent the pain.

Around 4 a.m. on January 5, 2015, he received a call from his dad. Joseph knew the news before he even answered. "I had felt it," he said. Without much elaboration, I knew exactly what Joseph meant; I had also felt it in me the day my dad died. Before even entering the hospital to learn the news, a jolt and then a tightening sensation in my stomach told me.

Upon seeing his mom's cold, lifeless body, Joseph pulled up a chair to hold her hand until he had to leave. "I don't know how long I sat there. All I remember is feeling like a large portion of me had left my body and only a shell had remained," he wrote. I had done the exact same thing; feeling lonely and hollow, I had held my dad's hand until we couldn't stay anymore. With shock, the minutes bore a certain viscosity, melting together into a massive blur.

When Joseph got home, he fell into bed, where he spent most of the following days. "I barely did anything but drink water and stare at the ceiling in confusion about my existence," he wrote. Emotionless and detached from the world, he was drowning in shock. Grief was sluggish. I had also spent the majority of that first week in bed, while people offered me water and food—a monotonous passage of time that felt so much like prison. Trapped inside my mind and left to survive.

Joseph spent most of high school evading grief. As he struggled to address his pain, the numbness prevented him from truly confronting his loss. "I didn't really feel much, but deep down, I was," he said. "I started feeling emotions that I didn't even know I had. It was every now and then in spurts, but it was definitely very much there, and it came out more graphically later on."

When he entered college, an intense depression exacerbated the grief. He had been harboring years of heartache, a festering wound buried just underneath the numbness. "I had depression throughout my childhood," he said, "but I just didn't really realize it."

When Joseph finally acknowledged his grief and began feeling the severity of his depression, he started searching for outlets to soothe the emptiness. He discovered solace in spending time alone, sometimes driving aimlessly or going out to listen to live music. "It made me realize how much you need to think about what's going on in your head," he said. "I never really imagined how much you would need to do that as a kid, but looking back, it's very obvious that you need to keep track of how you're feeling and sometimes really challenge the way you think. Although being alone can be stigmatized as a bad thing in our society, it is something I've begun to appreciate. It's made me confront where I am in life and where I want to be."

Eventually, he came across a service program at school where he began volunteering each week at a veterans' homeless shelter. His interactions with the men there helped Joseph better process his grief, as many of the men were working through their own issues, including loss. Over time, getting to know the veterans and hearing their stories gave him a renewed sense of hope. "I have become a different person," he told me. "Volunteering built this sense of connection in me I had never really felt before. There's something incredibly special about spending time with people completely different than you and sharing each other's battles in life."

Joseph and I shared our changed perspectives, which were similar. Relearning our relationships, becoming more spontaneous, contemplating death all the time—we were both ceaselessly working to figure out who we were supposed to be. Joseph was working at a window coverings company, a job he felt was greatly influenced by his mom and her love for home improvement projects. However, like me, he could sense there was more in store for him. "I'm still in the discovery mode," he said, and I told him I was too. Loss had sparked the unearthing of various passions for us both. We were searching for happiness in music, writing, and new opportunities, because we were armed with an instinct that this life was brimming with possibilities.

My developing connection with Joseph felt beautifully ironic. The two of us had encountered each other in solitude, our stories overlapping when we were most alone. We hardly knew each other, and yet, we did; the miles between us paled in comparison to the understanding that brought us together, all on the whim of a choice, a phone call, an email. In all the places where I felt incomplete, I knew Joseph felt incomplete too. Together we were emerging from the wreckage of loss, crawling out of our cocoons, and racing toward the infinite sky ahead.

A MESSAGE IN MUSIC
"Golden Embers" by Mandolin Orange

CHAPTER 21

THE BEGINNING
OF THE ROAD

───

I believe that because of this year, I will never be the same person again. My heart has been hardened and shattered and fused back together time and time again. I am broken, but in the kind of way that lets the light shine through the cracks. The year has ended, and I am just beginning. I will give life another chance. I am terrified. I am determined. I am brave.

—JANUARY 1, 2019, A PROMISE TO MYSELF

I gripped the steering wheel, speeding down our local parkway, with all four windows exposing me to the frigid air. Where I was going, I didn't know, but driving home was not an option. The only acceptable destination was nowhere; I would keep cruising through neighborhood streets and city main roads until I realized why.

These independent drives with no clear objective were almost always accompanied by music. This time, the sound of the wind was enough. I stuck my arm out the window and gripped the outside roof of the car. The metal was cold, and the tiny hairs stood up on my arm. Eyes on the road, mind in a trance, a strange intuition guiding me from one turn to the next. My dad's words surfaced in my mind.

Find your passion, do what you love, and you'll never work a day in your life.

I could see the outline of his figure so clearly, leaning against our off-white, textured walls. There had been an unmistakable sincerity in those eyes, ones I had teasingly labeled "beetle-black eyes" as a kid. They were really a deep, compelling shade of brown, framed by the faint lines of compassionate crow's feet. I tried to link his voice to the image, to form one continuous, holistic memory of his being, but all elements felt disconnected from each other, separate entities.

With the gas pedal under my foot and limitless road ahead, I contemplated my dad's advice. Discovering passion and purpose was his unshakable philosophy on life, his greatest value, and his irrefutable words of wisdom. From an early age, he instilled this idea in my head, and all these years later, it still held true.

I had not yet arrived at that destination of certainty, but I was certainly nearing something. Driving, thinking, evolving, I was approaching the next unknown chapter.

Drifting past different places reminded me how much I had changed. I could see a little girl in a plaid uniform jumper, chasing her classmates around the blacktop at recess. A gangly, awkward freshman huddling with her friends on the bleachers for her first football game. A girl aimlessly steering a black Saturn Ion down the main road. I was not who I used to be.

Weaving through streets I had traveled my entire life, my city felt like a time capsule; all the coffee shops, soccer fields, and middle school hangouts from my past were now just images in my rearview mirror.

Loss was filled with emotions I still didn't understand and words I might never find, but the pursuit to keep growing from the depths of my grief was endless. The people in my life had changed me—from Maryland to Texas to Spain to the room across from my dorm—and there were still more people to come. I wasn't finished hurting, or changing, or growing, and well . . . I never will be. This was the endless cycle. Hurting so hard we grow, loving so much we rise.

With my forearm still hanging out the window, the moment willed me into the strangest emotion: silent, happy tears and a sentimental knot in my stomach. It overtook me entirely. Suddenly, my arm was numb to the wind, accompanied by a fluttering sensation in my chest. Something I had never experienced before—a physical manifestation—my dad's presence enveloped me. Through tears, I laughed. He was there. I knew it. I could feel it.

With the glowing sliver of a moon lighting the road ahead of me, I knew that angels didn't miss what they left behind because they never left.

At once I knew, with everything in my being, that there are no true endings in life, only transitions. Only stories, where one chapter fades into another, where one universe becomes another, from the earthly to the eternal. Between these milestones are lessons, lessons that bring us to our knees. But this is loss. This is life. This is love. And among all these moments are smaller victories, where we learn to get up, start over, and keep moving toward the promise that life is far from over.

I inhaled the air, loosening my grasp on the steering wheel, leaning back to catch a glimpse of the moon.

There are infinite beginnings, and maybe this is one.

A MESSAGE IN MUSIC:
"Guiding Light" by Foy Vance

EPILOGUE

___

As I was nearing the end of this book, the weight of grief, stress, and that inevitable question of "is this even good enough?" loomed over the final months. I began to question the integrity of my writing and the entire reason I started this massive undertaking. Balancing work, school, and social life while writing a novel . . . let's just say you have to go into a cave for a couple months.

While I found myself in this "cave," on the brink of quitting, staring at the same sentence and blinking cursor for hours on end, I came across a note that completely grounded me and pushed me toward the final stages. Wandering into my bedroom one night, I arbitrarily pulled a book from my shelf: Natalie's Poetry, Volume I. This was a collection of poems (written by my eight-year-old self) that my parents had put together as a Christmas gift for me in second grade. From an early age, I loved to write, almost obsessively, and with scraps of computer paper or spare notepads, I scribbled words and tried to rhyme them. The poems in this book are hilariously indicative of my age at that time, so I'll spare you the details, but

I remember thinking it was the coolest gift ever, and honestly, it still is. I flaunted it to all my friends, brought it for show-and-tell, and carried it around in my backpack during the day, because who doesn't love a second-grade narcissist? The book was complete with an author bio (with a black and white picture of me smiling through my two crooked front teeth), a table of contents, and even what I considered a fancy copyright page. The book felt legit. At eight years old, I believed I was an author.

What made my discovery thirteen years later so monumental was that I had almost no recollection of the contents when I opened it. I grabbed it from the shelf, flipped to the end, and found the dedication page, written by my dad.

This book is dedicated to you Natalie. May all your dreams come true and you fully realize the talent and ability God has gifted you with. You are now a published author. The world impatiently waits for more of your humor, creative writing, and playful spirit. Always reach for the stars and never let go of your dreams. Mom and I can't wait to read more books from you. You are so wonderfully talented and gifted. We are so proud of you and the person you are becoming. Always pursue your passion and what you love, and you'll never work a day in your life.

Love,
Mom and Dad
Xoxoxoxoxoxoxoxoxoxoxoxoxoxoxoxoxoxoxoxoxoxoxoxooxo

As if he were speaking straight from Heaven to my heart, I read the dedication page about ten more times. Then I taped it to my bathroom mirror and told myself I would read those words every single day for the rest of my life.

My parents on their eighteenth wedding anniversary.
They were married for twenty years.

Family vacation in the Wisconsin Dells, 2008

ACKNOWLEDGMENTS

This book would not have been possible without the endless love and support from my mom, Dominic, Gabe, Luke, and the rest of my family and friends. You know who you are, and you know how much I love you.

The making of this book was built on the passion, entrepreneurial creativity, and limitless confidence of Eric Koester, Creator Institute and professor of practice, Georgetown University's McDonough School of Business; Brian Bies, head of publishing, New Degree Press, whose dedication and efficiency challenged me to keep writing; Stephen Howard, my developmental editor, who fearlessly supported my vision and fortified my belief in myself; Linda Berardelli, my incredible marketing editor, who guided the growth of this novel; and everyone at New Degree Press who works tirelessly to instill the skills and confidence in new writers of every kind.

To all those I interviewed for this book: your stories have changed me and given life to these pages.

With gratitude to Professor Kaitlin Creadon, who opened a door for me and taught me the power of writing something every day.

I am indebted to my Aunt Ann, who designed the cover of this book with uninhibited creativity and love.

A special thank you to Michelle Finnegan, Tess Murphy, and Margot Dunn, my undying sources of strength and unofficial editors; thank you for pushing my creative limits and eagerly refining my writing.

With love, for Abby Lutz, Mick Scanlon, Molly Penn, Emily Miller and Madeline Taphorn for being lights in my life.

To the readers of this book, for listening to my story and making it to the end.

I would also like to acknowledge my earliest supporters, those who have generously contributed to this experience and stood behind me from the very beginning:

Jill Sanchez	Kamila Cwanek
Erin Meilhon	Audra Malloy
Eric Sanchez	Ellie Fischer
Michael, Kathleen, and Molly Hodan	Cheryl and Larry Kooiman
Lee Anne and Jake Chappelle	Lauren and Peter Lawinger
Andy and Leslie Sanchez	Meghan McKale
Mady Swanstrom	Carla and Ray Wifler
Lisa Liljegren	Erika Gergits
Stephanie Franczak	Paige Haydin
Christine Sanchez	Frank DeGuire
Catherine Baranyk	Abby and Dave Barrett
Kevin and Emily Roethe	Olivia Homel
	Melissa Hatch
	Pam and Phil Foti

Kaitlyn O'Hair
Isabelle Shavlik
Ann Hilbert
Drew Schlidt
Angela Blamey
Jessica Elliott
Bridget Sullivan
Tracy Abler
Jen and Tim Sumiec
Jill, Ted, and Claire Hubley
John Niemer
Alyson and Randy Kaiser
Michael Velcherean
Tim Cigelske
Bill and Terri Lusk
Shelley and Mark Clausen
Kurt Schummer
Michele Schaefer
Barbara and John Deer
Anna Hemauer
Simba Gandari
Grace Devine
Sara French
Rebecca Huenink
Ellen, Rob, and
Abby Schlosser
Michele and Steve Harris
Colin Harris
Catherine and Dan Fleming
Erin and Jon Groth

Christy Blessing
Hannah Keller
Stephen and Claire Cady
Bob and Christy Maranan
Tom and Julie Antholine
Alyssa Mesa
Kimberly Phillips
Kelley Kornfeld
Lisa Metz
Jill VanTreeck
Nicole Zelazko
Garrett Trzcinski
Tina and Mike Andrew
Alex Shaw
Patrick Salter
Ally Parisi
Angie and Mike Brannigan
Becky Kelly
Judie Gillespie
Katie MacDonald
Danielle MacInnes
Jen Hale
Daphne and Will Duffy
James and Allison Friel
Chris Pfankuch
Joseph Pfankuch
Molly Laughlin
Brett and Sheri Birschbach
Maria Read
Elizabeth and Dan Kurt

Tess Murphy
Lisa and Tim Winn
Kelly and Tim Parbs
Matt Ream
Jill and Dave Dohnal
Ann Narus
Jennifer and Michael Steiner
Madi Daleiden
Stephen Howard
Larisa and Mike Bowman
Margot Dunn
Laura and Doug Shears
Colleen and Bill Mullooly
Kate Kenney
Lori Tschetter
Vanessa and Brent O'Neil
Monica and John Norfolk
Natalie Norfolk
Sheila Freeman
Leslie and Tony Colvin
Tom and Debbie Kerr
Kerry Martin
Margaret Thew
Gael Garbarino Cullen
Molly Stamper
Jenni Solomon
Michelle and Steve Pape
Carrie and Jason Kelroy
Karen Pings
Susan Moynihan

Noreen Walsh
Alicia Bartz
Jess Taylor
Kelly Stamm
Brigid Hughes
Kira Baker
Margaret and Mario Powell
Shelly and Scott Koranda
Emily Koranda
Molly and Doug Bell
Jackie and Jim Powell
Cantrece Forest
Rebecca Lukomski
Sarah Pike
Carolyn and Ed Callahan
Lindsey and Brian Moloney
Jan Salzmann
Stan and Edie Birschbach
Staci and Jay Salzmann
Marie Roderick
Katie Long
Liz Preston
Nastazsa Barrett
Shelley Haus
Jack Condit
James Harwood
Molly and Pete Holsen
Adrianne and Greg Busch
Jennifer Roehl
Jacqueline Hammond

Colleen and Chris Leffler
Kathleen Cullen and
Patrick Ritter
Brian Sanchez
Danny Pavlovich
Theresa and James Alioto
Mary and Chip Bunzel
Heidi and Tom Martin
Jason Beugnet

Mary Helen and
Steve Schulte
Libby Schulte
Ann and Marc Edmunds
Michelle and Sean Finnegan
Eric Koester
Kathleen Romfoe
Beverly Kreul

APPENDIX

———

INTRODUCTION
Merriam-Webster. s.v. "heal." Accessed February 8, 2020.
https://www.merriam-webster.com/dictionary/heal

CHAPTER 1
Lewis, C. S. A Grief Observed. Harper Collins. 1996

CHAPTER 3
Peart, Neil. Ghost Rider: Travels on the Healing Road. ECW Press. 2002.

CHAPTER 5
Cacciatore, Joanne. Bearing the Unbearable: Love, Loss, and the Heartbreaking Path of Grief. Wisdom Publications. 2017

Cacciatore, Joanne. "The Kindness Project." In Grief Therapy: Creative Practices for Counseling the Bereaved, edited by Robert A. Neimeyer, 329. New York: Routledge, 2012.

CHAPTER 7
Anderson, Jamie. "Jamie Anderson Quotes." Goodreads. Accessed February 1, 2020. https://www.goodreads.com/quotes/9657488-grief-i-ve-learned-is-really-just-love-it-s-all-the

CHAPTER 8
Angelo, Megan. "16 Unforgettable Things Maya Angelou Wrote and Said." Glamour. Accessed February 19, 2020. https://www.glamour.com/story/maya-angelou-quotes

CHAPTER 13
Krauss, Nicole. The History of Love. W.W. Norton & Company. 2005

CHAPTER 15
Peart, Neil. Ghost Rider: Travels on the Healing Road. ECW Press. 2002.

CHAPTER 18
Spielberg, Robin. Spa Piano. 2006, compact disc.

CHAPTER 19
Walter, Jennifer. "The day the music lived." Marquette University. Accessed January 9, 2020. https://stories.marquette.edu/the-day-the-music-lived-f51fa7bf9ac2

Printed in the USA
CPSIA information can be obtained
at www.ICGtesting.com
JSHW080836310124
55951JS00015B/129/J